LOOK AT THIS

Art Dwight

Tagral Media
TAGRALMEDIA.COM

PRAISE FOR *LOOK AT THIS*

"So many messages of this nature are presented from a 'perfect person' perspective, which makes it hard to relate. The vulnerability Art reveals in his stories makes me feel like I'm right there with him, like it's happening to me too!"

—Yvonne Bean

"These stories really hit home. I laughed, cried, reflected, and pondered on the circumstances in my own life and feel more at peace than I have in a long time."

—Terri Hannold

"I find Art's willingness to share his own honest experiences and resulting insights to be powerful examples of how to move gracefully through the ups and downs that life provides. Art does this in a non-threatening, non-preaching way that allows me to take what I need from his life lessons."

—David Slye

"The humor is great, the honesty greater, and the message is the greatest."
—Scott Rippey

"Art's willingness to share real-life issues and problems—to take an honest look at his own side of the street—is reassuring and inspiring."
—Jay King

"I love how Art puts himself in his stories and shows that he is not infallible. It makes us all feel better about ourselves because we all make mistakes, but with practice we can keep them from happening again."
—Camille Koscis

"Art's stories have inspired me to pause and reflect on what really matters. It is so easy to get caught up in the 'noise' of our daily lives, but his messages help me reflect on my purpose and why it matters. This book has been a great blessing and gift to me."
—Danielle White

"These stories speak to the heart of our shared human experience—they separate the wheat from the chaff—revealing what really matters in life."

—Amy Benton

"I love the transparency, honesty and insight into real life issues—and how our actions and decisions affect others around us."

—Jeff Burton

"Every message resonates with me and helps me look at the decisions I make in an entirely new way."

—Suzanne Rosetti

"The honesty, humor and relevance of Art's stories remind me of what's really important—and that the little lessons are there in each moment if I'm willing to look."

—Betsy Ingersoll

"Art's stories teach life lessons, heal guilt and make me laugh! It is comforting to know that we are all humans going through a shared human experience. No one is perfect—and that's okay."

—Leigh Mills

"These little nuggets of wisdom give me insight and common sense solutions to everyday problems."

—Brian Long

"Art has an innate ability to take the most mundane experience and find the meaning behind it."

—Eliot Pfanstiehl

"Inspirational! I can relate to Art's stories because it resonates with my own life experiences and he always has a better way of looking at any situation."

—Marcus Dowd

Contact Art
www.ArtDwight.com

Look at This

Printed in the United States of America
First Edition, October 2011

ISBN 978-0-9839418-0-4

Published by Tagral Media

Cover Design by 1106 Design

Author Notes

ANY OF THE STORIES in this book are drawn from and inspired by my immediate family: my wife, Raquel Bono, step daughter, Taylor Bono, and my daughters, Grace and Aly Dwight.

Although the stories are true, in some instances I omitted names, used only first names, or changed names to respect their privacy.

Acknowledgments

SPECIAL THANKS TO my editor Emily Krump, whose guidance, experience and corrections were invaluable; Tony and Rose Cruz for providing the background on *A True Sailor;* Don Dwight for his photo journalism of my childhood; Laura Dwight for her photographic expertise; and most of all, Raquel, whose boundless support, patience and love made it all possible.

Contents

Just Finish the Job

A moment's insight is sometimes worth a lifetime of experience.
—OLIVER WENDELL HOLMES

◦—·—▷◁◦▷◁—·—◦

I DON'T KNOW IF IT WAS A SOPHOMORE SLUMP or academic burnout; all I do know is that I hated second grade. I tried every trick in the "How to Avoid School" manual on Mom, but nothing worked. Then one day it hit me: If I "accidentally" miss the bus, I miss school. It was such a brilliant idea I couldn't believe I hadn't thought of it before.

The next morning, I put my plan into action. I walked to the bus stop as if heading toward my execution. Kids were still boarding the bus as I approached, so I hid behind a tree and watched until the bus departed. As it disappeared from view, however, I started to panic. My scheme didn't account for what came next. I was wading into uncharted waters. One moment I was an ordinary kid, and the next, a seven-year-old criminal.

Walking home, I quickly rehearsed my story as I prepared to face my mother.

Gee, Mom, can you believe it? The bus left early. What could I do? What could she say? *Oh, you poor thing, let me turn on the TV for you and get you some snacks.* When I walked into the kitchen, however, she took one look at me and read me like a cheap novel.

1

Furious, she made a phone call and two minutes later I was a prisoner in the back of our Ford Country Squire station wagon. Although Mom had ignored my desperate pleas to turn around, I had no intention of giving up that easily when we arrived. But when she pulled into the cul-de-sac, I saw the school principal waiting for us and I understood the purpose of her phone call with horrifying clarity. She had already anticipated my next move.

I see how it is, I thought, *sold out by my own mother. Fine, but I'm not going down without a fight.* The principal opened the door to pull me out of the car, but I clung to the door handle like my life depended on it. He finally succeeded in separating me from the car, locked me in a bear hug and dragged me to class as I kicked, wriggled, twisted and screamed the entire way.

When he opened the door to the classroom, my teacher stopped talking and all eyes turned to me, standing there in the doorway with tears streaming down my red face. I was humiliated. Nothing had gone according to plan.

This incident, however, did not kill my determination to skip school—it inflamed it. It's been said that crazy ideas are born of desperate minds. I was desperate, but I needed an irrefutable reason, something that my parents couldn't ignore. I had to find a way to actually get sick.

I found the solution in the woods behind my house. I was with my best friend Chris when I spotted a tree teeming with poison oak. *I'm hyper-allergic to this stuff,* I thought, *there's no way I'm going to school if I get a really bad case of it.* With the skill of a radical terrorist convincing a recruit that thirty pounds of high explosives strapped to their body is a noble endeavor, I persuaded him to join my masochistic mission.

"Let's do this," I said as I grabbed handfuls of the poisonous leaves. It was obvious that Chris still had some cognitive function as he tentatively rubbed the leaves onto his arms. As for me, I went nuclear. *I'll show that principal a thing or two.* I forcefully rubbed the poison oak onto my body and face as if it would somehow erase the shame of crying in front of my class.

The next morning, I woke up in agony—my body was an itchy, inflamed, grotesque mess. My eyes were swollen to the size of golf balls. My parents, clueless that it was a self-inflicted condition, kept me out of school for a week and lavished me with sympathy, attention, and get-well gifts. But I was so miserable I would've done anything to be healthy—even if it meant going back to school. If we had the internet back then "Poison Oak Boy" would've surely gone viral as one of the top ten dumbest acts of 1967.

Twelve years later I saw an eerily similar replay of my poison oak caper, but this time as a witness, not a participant. I was in Marine Corps basic training when two of my platoon members, desperate to be discharged, faked a suicide attempt with a Trac II razor. They didn't get their wish to be released. In fact, they got their worst nightmare: they were ordered to start basic training over *from the beginning.*

After this incident, our senior drill instructor addressed the platoon. "Men, if you want to leave Parris Island you can try to swim through the swamps and take your chances with the alligators or you can do something stupid like two of your platoon mates just did, but let me give you some advice, the easiest way off this island is to graduate. Just finish the job."

I finally got it. Those simple words made so much sense. There were times during basic training when I felt like I couldn't take it anymore, but trying to quit would only compound my problems. My drill instructor was right—the easiest way out, no matter how hard, is to buckle down and finish the job.

The only antidote for any obligation or responsibility is action. To help me keep this habit I read a card every morning that reads: SHOW UP FOR LIFE TODAY. NO WHINING. NO COMPLAINING. NO EXCUSES. JUST GET IT DONE. Nothing will ever happen unless

I make it happen. So whether it's writing this story, initiating a difficult conversation or even doing the dishes, I hear my drill instructor telling me to "Just finish the job." And I get right back to work.

With my Mom
South Hadley, Massachusetts–October 1967

Reaching for a Star (Fish)

A sister is a gift to the heart, a friend to the spirit,
a golden thread to the meaning of life.
—ISADORA JAMES

"I WANT THAT ONE!" my sister Ellie screamed just loudly enough to overcome the sounds of the crashing surf. I could see her pointing to the starfish she wanted, but I was hoping one of the dozens of closer starfishes would suffice.

"How about this one?" I shouted hopefully, pointing to one fifteen feet nearer as I struggled to keep my balance on the rocks.

"No! No! No! I want *that* one!" pointing again to the prized starfish, which revealed itself momentarily once the surf receded from a violent crash.

It was the summer of 1968. We were on a rock jetty extending far out from Laguna Beach, California. I was seven years old, Ellie a year older, or at least until October when her birthday widened the gap by two years. When that happened, I couldn't wait until my next birthday in May so I could put Ellie on notice that, once again, I was catching up to her. I acted like it was a competition, but the truth is that I just loved being closer to her.

5

I'm going to be honest with you, during those early years, we were adorable. We held hands, shared secrets and played games only we could understand. It was as if were genetically engineered to be playmates. To family, we were known as the "bear cubs." To me, Ellie was my best friend. I adored her and would've have done anything for her.

And so it was that Ellie wanted this big, fat juicy starfish, but unfortunately for me, it was right in the heart of Poseidon's kill zone. I was determined to get it for her, but the waves were rapidly growing in size, speed and strength. What we didn't know was that an undersea shift had created a massive disturbance along the entire Los Angeles coast line, resulting in dangerous rip tides and rogue waves almost twelve feet high.

Ellie gave no sign of changing her mind, so I pressed on. The cycle of the crashing surf gave me just enough time to jump to one boulder at a time. I had to wrap my arms around each rock, hold my breath, and hang on so the undertow wouldn't pull me out to sea. When the wave receded enough for my head to clear the roiling waters, I could hear my personal cheerleader Ellie, "You can do it! You're almost there!"

She was right. I looked up and there it was—the mother of all starfishes. But as I stretched my arm out to grab it, a monster wave slammed into me and then into Ellie, trapping us between the gaps in the rocks. We were submerged and unable to break free. Suddenly, I felt strong arms pulling me out of the water as if God himself had personally dispatched angels from Heaven to save us. We had been rescued by California lifeguards long before Baywatch fame.

The next day, the headline of the *Los Angeles Times* read, "700 Surf Rescues: High Waves Swept Many Out To Sea." When I think of that day, I could conclude that I risked everything because I was naïve and didn't understand the risk. And while that's true, I think my underlying motivation was much simpler: I loved Ellie and I wanted to make her happy.

I think the love we had for each other was what love really is. My love for Ellie was innocent, pure, and true—a love that put her needs and interests above my own without regard for personal cost. It taught me that I don't need to look forward to finding love; I just have to look back to *remember* what it really is.

True love motivates me to do whatever has to be done simply because the person I love wants or needs it. Ellie really wanted that starfish. It didn't matter that it made no logical sense to risk my life for an echinoderm.

To this day, I can still see that starfish clinging to the rock with my hand just inches away from it. I still have some regret that I couldn't complete my quest, but I also feel satisfied because I know that I went all out. And if I ever have the chance again, I'll get her that starfish.

Just because I love her.

With Ellie and the *LA Times*
Laguna Beach, California–July 1967

"The Bear Cubs"
South Hadley, Massachusetts–1965

A Key to Freedom

If you're going to seek revenge, you had better dig two graves.
—CHINESE PROVERB

W HEN I STARTED SEVENTH GRADE, despite an inferiority complex, a pathological fear of rejection and limited social skills, I was a healthy, well-adjusted twelve-year-old boy. I was convinced that everyone else was smarter, funnier, more attractive, popular and athletic than me, a hypothesis validated by the Darwinian meat market of picking teams, where I was almost always the last one chosen. I was a perfect target for ostracism and on the first day of school, I got it.

The five meanest kids in school kicked off a two-year campaign of harassment, intimidation, name calling and physical abuse. The bullies were led by a boy named Ricky, who seemed to have only one goal in life; to destroy me, to inflict as much pain as he possibly could. When he looked at me, his eyes blazed with contempt and hatred as if my existence were the cause of it and my destruction the only cure.

Years later, I often wondered why Ricky chose me as his target. It did not help that my father was the lieutenant governor of Massachusetts, but in fairness to my dad, I think my pants may have been the catalyst. On the first day of school, I wore a pair of striped polyester, bellbottom pants that were so hideous, even when I look at that photo today, I feel like beating myself up.

After that, every day was a struggle for survival, especially between classes. As the minutes ticked down toward the bell, I had to decide which route to take, whether to stay longer in class, take my chances walking closely behind other students, or hide in the bathroom and risk losing an escape route.

Whenever Ricky or one his hoodlum friends saw me, they morphed into gleeful, demonic hunters who had just spotted their prey. Words such as geek, loser, fag, wimp, dork, or queer were their primary weapons, preceded by "Dwight is a..." to ensure everyone knew who they were talking about, followed by maniacal laughter that cut deeper than a switchblade. Breaking into my locker to steal my lunch or anything else they could grab happened so routinely it felt like part of the curriculum.

They coordinated their physical attacks like velociraptors. They would divert my attention from my front or flanks, allowing another to hit me from behind with elbows to the head, kidney punches or body slams into the wall. I loved baseball, but quit the team after they jumped me while I was running laps around the school.

I learned to cope with the temporary physical pain, but the emotional pain grew like a malignant cancer in my mind. The shame and ignominy of knowing that everyone else heard it too was devastating, but the real source of my hurt, I later discovered, was that I believed it too.

I left junior high in 1975, and I never saw Ricky again, but the memories continued to torment me and the psychological wounds would not heal. Just the name, *Ricky*, was an epithet that ignited rage and a passion for vengeance. I hated him. I wanted to hurt him. I didn't know that the only person I was hurting was me.

I learned the hard way, that hate is a terribly self-destructive animal.

After one year of college I enlisted in the Marine Corps in hopes of finding some direction in my life, and unconsciously, as an outlet for the anger still burning within me. On the first day of boot camp, one of the drill instructors singled me out for special treatment and punished the entire platoon for my mistake. This incensed a fellow recruit, Chris, who never let me forget it.

Throughout boot camp, he relentlessly made sarcastic comments about my intelligence, qualifications or competence. What he couldn't know was that he was opening up old wounds—causing me to relive the pain and trauma of junior high. In my mind, as the verbal attacks escalated, Chris was gradually becoming Ricky.

About a week before graduation, I hit my breaking point. We were in the bathroom shaving when Chris said something that put me over the edge. I threw him into the wall and punched him repeatedly, unleashing six years of repressed rage. When he slumped to the floor, I straddled his chest and started choking him with all my strength. It took at least six recruits to pull me off him.

When I saw his tomato-red face and the purple imprints my hands left on his throat, I felt sick. If my platoon hadn't intervened, I could've killed him. Chris made one final comment, spoken very softly through strained vocal chords, "Man, that guy's crazy." And he never said another word to me. But he was right, in that moment, I *was* crazy. Although it was cathartic to overcome my fear and "be a man," I solved nothing.

By attacking Chris I had become what I loathed and despised. In that moment, I knew what it felt like to be Ricky. I could see that what drove Ricky wasn't hate, but pain. And as difficult as my childhood was, his was likely much worse. We were both suffering—we just handled it differently.

The compassion I felt for Ricky helped release the self-destructive anger and resentment that I had been harboring for so long. I didn't know it at the time, but this was my first experience with forgiveness. My inability to forgive Ricky was keeping me trapped in junior high school. I was nineteen years old, but emotionally I was still thirteen, scared, insecure and vulnerable. I couldn't grow up until I let go.

I could forgive Ricky because I finally learned how to forgive myself. And in a larger sense, I learned that my fight was never with Ricky, it was with me. This is true of anyone I've ever held grievances against. If I can't sleep at night because I'm upset with someone else—it isn't affecting that person—it's only causing problems for me. A *Course in Miracles* says that, "Forgiveness is the key to happiness," but would add that for me, forgiveness is the key to emotional freedom and peace of mind. It doesn't matter how much I've been hurt or how severe the transgression—forgiveness is the only way out.

With my brother Stuart, left, first day of school
Wayland, Massachusetts–1973

A Hike to Remember

*The whole process of mental, spiritual and material
riches may be summed up in one word: Gratitude.*
—JOSEPH MURPHY

———— ✥✥✥ ————

WHEN I WAS FOURTEEN-YEARS-OLD, my parents presented me
with an opportunity to attend a two-week backpacking course
in Wyoming's Wind River Range. It wasn't explicitly stated, but I
don't think it was optional. Considering my behavior at the time, I
suspected that other alternatives, such as military school or a juvenile
correctional institution, were under consideration. With that in mind,
I jumped at the National Outdoor Leadership School (NOLS).

It was only two weeks, how hard could it be?

After ten days of wilderness training, rock climbing, and backpacking we were divided into groups of six for a survival hike—a
three-day exercise living off the land while navigating our way out
of the mountains without our instructors. The hike was fine, but
seventy two hours without food wasn't going to work for me so I
squirreled away food in my backpack. Just before we left, however,
our instructors did a shake-down of our equipment and confiscated
my stash. I started to think that I should have paid closer attention
during survival training.

My concern escalated to panic when my group elected me as the leader. "Are you crazy?" I asked my friend David, who we called Moses, "I got us lost on a training hike!"

"I know that," he agreed, "but we had to make sure Allen didn't get it." Allen had the skills of Daniel Boone, but he was so arrogant that no one could stand him. No matter what I said, I could not persuade them to pick another leader.

My first order of business was to plot a route that took us by a plethora of lakes where, according to my brilliant plan, fish would be jumping out of the water and into our frying pans. As we soon found out, though, these "lakes" were either too small or dried out for us to catch fish. My route of plenty had quickly become a death march.

By the second night after hiking more than fifteen miles without food, a primal, gnawing hunger grew like a pernicious virus within us. We were no longer six kids on a wilderness adventure; we were a feral mob on a toboggan ride into anarchy. I didn't know how close we were to cannibalism, but given my rapidly declining approval ratings, I feared I would be the first to go.

In desperation we gathered the edible flowers and plants we had been trained to identify, but when it came time to eat the stuff raw, we just couldn't do it. The time had come for me to lead. I proposed that we boil the stuff in water with spices to make "flower stew."

As everyone filled their bowls with the funky, watery mixture I had a flash of hope, *this might actually work*. I'm not sure when it all went wrong; maybe it was when we discovered it was the most revolting thing we'd ever tasted, or perhaps it was two minutes later when we were on our knees violently barfing.

Afterward, I couldn't help but notice the *I hate you with the white-hot intensity of a thousand suns* look in their wild, hungry eyes. As foul as it was, I think that stew may have saved me. Even if they wanted to go *Lord of the Flies* on me, the group was too exhausted to do anything about it. And the experience strengthened my bond with Moses, who whispered to me later that night, "Let's not ever tell anyone about this."

On the morning of the fourth day our mangy, starving band found its way to the meeting point. As we broke through the woods into the clearing, the sight of the yellow NOLS bus was the happiest moment of my young life. I never imagined a school bus could bring me that much joy.

We were given a choice of cereals and it was *Cheerios* for me. That simple bowl of cereal was a euphoric culinary experience; every grain tasted like heaven's oats, the sugar sweeter than anything I've ever tasted, and the milk, the nectar of the gods. It was an experience so powerful that I savor that thirty-five-year-old memory like it was today.

Since the day I was born, until NOLS, I had lived about 4,745 days and eaten roughly 14,235 consecutive meals without ever missing one. It took just three days, or just nine missed meals, for me to appreciate how lucky I am to eat abundantly every day. I don't always follow my own counsel here, but I should: every meal is a cause for celebration, appreciation, and gratitude. One good meal a day makes me more fortunate than one billion people on this earth who are starving, malnourished, or dying.

Gratitude is born of experience. When my parents used the, "Think of the starving kids around the world," line when I didn't finish my dinner, it just didn't do it for me. But when I went *three days* without eating, I learned how fortunate I am in a way that a thousand stories or lectures never could.

My experience at NOLS was the first time I learned how important adversity is to learning, for without it I would never change or grow. When I'm faced with difficult circumstances, instead of feeling sorry for myself, I've learned to be grateful for them. Some devout Buddhists believe in the value of suffering so much that they *ask* for it. I get that, but I'm content to let the so-called good times roll for as long as life allows. The trials will come and when they do, I know they will help me become a better person.

And for that, I am now, and always will be, abundantly grateful.

Me, Benton Street and John Crody
Wind River Range, Wyoming–July 1974

The Day I Met Jesus

To believe in the things you see and touch is no belief at all;
but to believe in the unseen is a triumph and a blessing.
—ABRAHAM LINCOLN

NE DAY, I SEE MYSELF as a grandfather, sitting on my front porch on a warm and sunny summer day, telling my grandkids stories of my youth. One of my favorites begins like this, "Did I ever tell you about the time I met Jesus?"

"Did you really meet Jesus, Grandpa?" they'd ask, eyes wide with excitement and wonder.

"Well, kids," I begin, "You'll have to decide that for yourselves, but here is my story …"

During my senior year at Deerfield Academy, at the time an all-boy prep school nestled in the Pocumtuck Valley of Western Massachusetts, I was in a small group of upperclassmen who enjoyed the coveted perk of eating in the cafeteria instead of mandatory sit-down dinners. This privilege was usually reserved for students with high academic or athletic standing, so I'm not sure why I was chosen for this honor, but I had enough sense to never question it.

After dinner one soft, warm September evening, I used my small slice of freedom from prep school life to walk down to the Deerfield River, which meandered along a stretch of thin woods at the far edge of the lower level, a lush and verdant expanse of athletic fields.

As I entered the woods I sensed that something was out of place, but nothing could prepare me for what came next. After taking a few more steps I was shocked to see a long-haired man with his back to me, sitting motionless on a rock, looking out at the river. In four years I had never seen anyone not associated with the school down here. The fact that this guy was here was bizarre enough. It was about to get weirder.

With his back still to me, he spoke softly saying something like this, "The river only flows one way. It doesn't resist or fight what it cannot control." *Okay butthead*, I thought, *first of all, you're in my spot. Second, what kind of drug-induced, hippie-speak is that?* As if he could hear my thoughts, he slowly turned his head around, looked directly into my eyes and said with calm authority, "For you see, I am Jesus Christ."

I didn't see that one coming.

This was a tough sentence to process on its own merit, but what was really freaking me out is that he was speaking in parables and despite the blue jeans, he looked exactly like Jesus. Or, at least how we've imagined he might look; a thin man with deep, dark, mesmerizing brown eyes, a mustache and a beard.

He kept his eyes locked on mine like Star Trek tractor beams as I quickly weighed my options. And in my mind, there were only two. This guy was very likely psychotic—a knife-wielding Charles Manson disciple who was about to spring from the rock and go Helter Skelter on me, slicing me into a dozen pieces. On the other hand, I couldn't rule out the five-hundred-trillion-to-one chance that this man was who he said he was.

If he *was* a nut job, I wondered, could I take this guy? I thought about going Chuck Norris on him—dropping him like a bad habit with one lightning-fast, spinning round-house kick to the head. Unfortunately, there was a flaw in that plan. I didn't know karate— and I didn't think my training regimen of tennis, hockey, and dorm wrestling could compensate for that.

If he really was Jesus, however, the prospect of spiritual account-ability was alarming. That would mean he already knew about the butthead remark, the crudely-wrapped "cigarette" in my back pocket and my plan to knock him out. I already had enough problems with school authorities, I didn't need this. But what could I say? "Hey Jesus, don't get me wrong, I appreciate the visit, but this isn't a good time for me. Could we reschedule?"

I felt like I was getting a brain hernia as his eyes continued to hold mine with a steady, peaceful, near-paralyzing gaze. It felt like hours, but likely took seconds for fear to make my decision for me. I reluctantly broke free of his gaze, turned, and ran like Roger Bannister on amphetamines, not stopping until I reached the main campus just as my classmates were pouring out of the dining hall.

Breathless and jacked up on adrenaline, I ran into a group of my friends and blurted out, "You're not going to believe this, but there's a guy down by the river who says he's Jesus."

"Let's go kick his ass!" exclaimed my classmate Jim. *Oh that's just great*, I thought, *not only have I blown any chance of absolution, but I'm the first person to see Jesus in two thousand years and the first thing I'm going to do is get his ass kicked by a bunch of reprobate, testosterone-fueled preppies.*

We rushed down to the spot where he was only to find that he was gone. I was both relieved and humiliated. Jesus wasn't going to get pummeled by preppies. But I could already hear the ridicule that might follow me to graduation, like, "Hey, Art! Seen Jesus lately?" Or worse, with a nickname I hated and could not shake, "Hey, Bullwinkle, got Jesus?"

It's been more than thirty years since that moment by the Deerfield River and I've often wondered what might have happened had I stayed.

I loved the story and I wanted to share it, but I struggled to find the meaning. I originally wrote this a year ago—and just yesterday the answer came to me and it was so obvious I couldn't believe it eluded me for so long.

It was what he said about the river.

By comparing life to the river, he was sharing the secret of how my life should be. Like everything in life, the river never rests. It is always moving, changing and adapting. When it encounters rocks or other obstacles, it never resists them; it just flows effortlessly around them and keeps moving on its way. It lives in harmony with itself and everything in its environment.

Me? Not so much.

Far too many times when something didn't go my way, instead of accepting it gracefully or moving around it like the river, I'd fight it. When someone didn't agree with me, I tried to change their opinion instead of allowing it to just be. I learned the hard way that I can no sooner change other people than I could stop the sun from rising in the east. Clinically speaking, trying to control things I can't control is insane.

The river, however, has no knowledge of this kind of self-created conflict or stress. Unlike me, it doesn't have "issues" with other people. It doesn't try to change things it cannot change. Even when it's been poisoned by fertilizers or other toxic chemicals, it doesn't fight back, struggle or whine about how unfair it is—it simply continues to live its life the best, and only way, it can.

In the end, the only difference between me and the river is that I have a choice. I can choose to learn from what the river teaches me and live in peace and harmony regardless of my life circumstances, or I can resist and fight my life situation, resulting in drama, suffering and unhappiness. And maybe, just maybe, that's what "Jesus" was trying to say to me that day.

As I conclude my story, my grandchildren ask, "Do you think it was really Jesus, Grandpa?"

"I don't know, kids," I reply. "But I do know that every moment in life is a gift, a divine opportunity containing a lesson or truth waiting patiently for me to find it," and then I pause, concluding, "If he really was Jesus, I just hope there are no hard feelings about the butthead comment and that the first thing I hear when it's my time to go isn't, 'Mr. Dwight, about that day at the river...'"

A Whale of a Tale

Get the facts, or the facts will get you.
And when you get them, get them right.
—Dr. Thomas Fuller

————— ✳ —————

My Deerfield classmate, Steven "Whale" Wyman, is the funniest, most entertaining person I have ever known. A storytelling freak of nature, fueled by incomprehensible quantities of Tab soda smuggled in and stored in an illegal refrigerator (it was rumored he'd consume a case a day), he cranked out tales like a verbal machine gun, stopping only for a slug of Tab or to catch his breath. It was an extraordinary theatrical experience.

There was standing room only in "Whale's Theater" as classmates came to be entertained, informed or just marvel at Steve's seemingly inhuman stamina. He'd punch or slap classmates if he saw their attention drifting, which is why veteran patrons learned to stand in the back of the room. Classmates came and went, but Steve never stopped. I often wondered what happened when the last person left. Would he just stop? Keep going? Pass out? Would he even notice?

During one of these marathon sessions Steve said that the reason gin was known for creating mean drunks was because it was made from the juniper berry which has hallucinogenic properties. He bolstered his credibility by reminding us that his father was a liquor distributor. I bit like a trout. Call me stupid, naïve, gullible, but I never thought to question it.

From that moment on, whenever the conversation turned to alcohol, I often shared this little gin factoid with dozens, if not hundreds, of other people. During our twenty-fifth high school reunion, I told Steve how I never forgot what he told me about gin. That's when the affable man stopped, looked into my eyes and said with death-in-the-family seriousness, "Art, that was total bullshit."

"Oh, that's just great Whale," I said. "I've been selling that story for twenty-five years." It was bad enough that it wasn't true, but I told it like I was some kind of expert on the subject. Thanks to me and Steve (I'm not going to hang alone on this one), I wondered how many other people were spreading this story to gullible people like me.

I didn't have to wait long for my answer. Our friend Dan "Guppy" Goss, thusly nicknamed for the gills on his neck that grew from the hours he spent in the water with our New England champion swim team, joined our conversation. Apparently he's been telling the gin story for years too, instantly doubling the number.

While this gin mistruth is fairly harmless, so much of what we hear and share is not. In his book, *The Four Agreements*, Don Miguel Ruiz describes gossip as a virus that infects the person who accepts it as well as anyone who shares it. My moment with Steve put an exclamation point on Ruiz's wisdom and inspired me to create my own personal firewall for things that I hear or read.

When I hear opinions, judgments, or assumptions about people, things, or situations, I use a mental pop-up with one question, *Is it the truth?* This forces me to critically examine what I am hearing or reading. It helps me objectively reason, rather than just accept or react. It also helps me uncover blind spots in my thinking. I found that there were many things that I believed were true, but were actually things I *wanted* to be true, especially if I was emotionally tied to it.

From the time my daughters were young enough to comprehend English I told them that the rivalry between the Red Sox and the Yankees was much more than baseball—it was actually a struggle of good versus evil. The only comfort I can take from that faux pas is that I was convinced it was true. As Seinfeld's George Costanza said, "It isn't really lying, if you believe it."

I frequently receive forwarded email messages that contain shocking allegations about politicians, attributed to credible people. I used to react emotionally to these messages, with the outrage and shock they are intended to create, and would feel compelled to send on to others. But when I take a moment to ask myself if it's the truth, it allows logic to intervene. And when I research these stories, I find they are often misleading or entirely fabricated.

I've learned that the adage, "Don't believe everything you read or hear," means *exactly* what it says. It's my responsibility to apply reason, logic and facts to *everything* I read or hear. If I take a moment to think first—I help become part of the solution—and avoid personal embarrassment in the process. But what do I know? I just had a few gin and tonics; I think I may be hallucinating.

Steven "Whale" Wyman
Delray Beach, Florida–March 2007

True Kindness

There's no such thing as a small act of kindness.
Every act creates a ripple with no logical end.
—SCOTT ADAMS

⌐⋆⊟✦⊟⋆⌐

THE HARDEST WORDS I've ever heard were the ones that ended my
time as a Deerfield Academy student.

"You're out," Dean Jim Fabiani said. "And once you leave here,
you cannot return to this campus before graduation under any circumstances." It was a sudden and devastating end to my four years
at Deerfield only six weeks before graduation.

As for the decision to expel me, the only truly remarkable thing
was that it didn't happen sooner. Dean Fabiani and Headmaster David
Pynchon did everything in their power to save me, but leading the
Class of 1979 in busts, suspensions, and other shenanigans was too
much to overcome or overlook. If only Deerfield's motto had been
"Be *un*worthy of your heritage," my father would've been so proud.

Ironically, the end of my Deerfield career had nothing to do with
unauthorized female guests in the dorm, marginal grades, skipping
classes, underage drinking, stealing keys from the security office or
even wrecking a rental car after a night of high-speed car jumping.
It was an honor code violation. I lied.

As I left the Main School Building for the last time, the enormity of my situation hit me like an emotional avalanche. It seemed certain that this would nullify my acceptance to Hobart College, which meant that the future as I knew it ceased to exist. A painful combination of guilt, shame, anger and self-recrimination swept through me, but the worst part of it was leaving my classmates. To me, Deerfield was more than a school; it was my family and my home.

And now I would have to face my father in Minneapolis. I recalled with dread the ditty he so often shared with me, "Oh, what a tangled web we weave when at first we practice to deceive." It had just been fulfilled like a tragic Shakespearean prophecy. He was right, again.

When I arrived home I don't think my parents knew what to do with me—and I certainly didn't know what to do with myself. I had never felt so completely lost. I decided to go back East, where I felt like I belonged. When my parents wouldn't agree to pay for a flight, I played the only card I felt I had left:

"I'm eighteen, I'm leaving and you can't stop me."

"Fine, but you're not getting any help from us."

"Okay fine," I said, "I'm going to Boston."

I stormed upstairs, stuffed some clothes into my backpack and headed for the door. The finality of this move seemed to hit my parents pretty hard. My dad gave me my first ride to the Wisconsin border, where he dropped me off on an open stretch on I-94. Neither one of us knew what to say. There was nothing in either of our experiences to prepare us for this. He hugged me and gave me $200 cash. I was overwhelmed. It wasn't the money, although it was nice since I was broke, it was a feeling that he still cared for me at a time when I cared very little for myself.

As I watched my dad drive off I felt alone, but strangely free. After a lifetime of dependency, I was doing something on my own. What I was doing was crazy, dangerous and misguided, but for the first time I was taking charge of my own life. I stuck my thumb out at passing cars. I waited less than ten minutes before a big, green

American sedan pulled up and I received my indoctrination into hitchhiking protocol.

"So you're headed to Boston," he said.

"That's right," I replied.

"My girlfriend and I can take you as far as Chicago."

"That would be great!"

"Hop in!"

As we pulled away from the curb, I was excited but a little freaked out when the speedometer soared past one hundred miles per hour. I did something that my dad would actually be proud of, for the first time in my life I voluntarily buckled my seat belt. They seemed to enjoy living on the edge, but what surprised me was how interested and concerned they were about my welfare, my safety and my plans. I didn't know how to receive their generosity. *If only they knew the truth*, I thought, *I'm a crazy, desperate homeless man, with no school, no family and no future.*

When we arrived at their exit just north of Chicago, I was anxious to keep moving, but they insisted on buying me a steak dinner and warmer clothes. So we had our steak at Sambos (a restaurant chain back then, you can't make this stuff up) and we went to K-Mart where he bought me a warmer sweater. I was embarrassed by his generosity, but found it was easier to accept than resist. When he dropped me back off on the highway, he said he wasn't leaving until I accepted $50. I felt like I had just been adopted.

This hitchhiking thing isn't so bad, I thought, *I'm even making a profit.* My luck was about to change. I was about to learn my first lesson of hitchhiking; long-distance rides are tough to get when you're in a city, especially at night. Considering Chicago extends for about thirty miles, I was in for a long night. I waited in one spot for nearly six hours.

Finally, around three in the morning, I got a lift from a guy who promised me he'd get me through Chicago, but claimed he had to make a stop first. The stop he had in mind wasn't in a neighborhood—it was a war zone, replete with burned-out buildings, broken glass, graffiti and rubble. The few working streetlights cast an eerie light among the shadows. I felt certain I was the first preppy kid to ever set foot in this foreboding, dangerous world. And increasingly certain I would be the last.

He said he needed to see some friends and party for a while. He seemed nice enough, but pictures of being robbed, beaten and killed flashed through my mind. I considered dropping to my knees and begging him to take me back to the highway. If they jumped me, I decided my only hope was to give away everything I had (money, backpack, whatever) if they would just let me live. But when we entered the apartment a few minutes later, to my great relief, there actually was a party.

I remained frozen in a chair as the party raged in front of me. I promised myself, if I lived through this night, I would make changes. I didn't know what changes, but I knew that this wasn't working. I finally found the courage to ask my host for a ride back to the highway. "No problem," he said, but that he couldn't take me out of Chicago now because he was too messed up. When he dropped me off near an entrance ramp to I-90, I breathed a sigh of relief.

As dawn started to break, the curtain closed on the longest, scariest night of my life. I was alive and that alone felt really good. After a short wait a beat up truck pulled over. To my surprise, inside was a girl in her twenties wearing coke spoon earrings. I was about to get another surprise. She told me how LSD has changed her life. "It's the best, man," she said, and that she had three hits of blotter acid a few hours ago. I didn't know much about LSD, but that sounded like a lot. I later learned that it's enough to send an elephant to Mars.

She asked me where I was going and I told her that all I cared about was getting to the far side of Chicago. She said it was out of her way, but that she'd be happy to do it. At this point, I was so exhausted that I was willing to take my chances. When she dropped me off, she wished me luck and gave me $20. The way people kept doing that made me wonder *just how pathetic do I look?*

Unfortunately I soon learned that she left me in a spot that was nowhere near I-90, except, perhaps, in her universe. After a few more rides, I ended up on a two-lane road seemingly miles from anywhere. And that's when the rain started, the winds picked up and the temperature dropped. I shivered uncontrollably as exhaustion, fear and frustration took its toll. When the lettering on my EAST sign melted into an unrecognizable smudge, I started breaking down.

It was here that I learned my second lesson in hitchhiking: wet, scary-looking, emotionally-broken people don't get picked up on back roads. Three hours and hundreds of cars passed without slowing down. I started having desperate, crazy thoughts, like calling my parents for help. As if in answer to my prayers, a van pulled up driven by an elderly couple.

When I told them I was trying to head east to Boston, she said, "Honey, you're in Michigan." They told me not to worry and that they would get me to Route 90, but that it would take about an hour and a half to "get me straightened out." I laughed to myself for the first time in weeks, thinking it would take a lot more than ninety minutes to straighten me out.

They gave me hot tea, cookies and even had a curtain where I could change out of my wet clothes into clothes from my backpack, also wet, but drier than what I was wearing. After ministering to my physical needs, she read passages from the Bible to me the rest of the trip. Some might label this couple as missionaries, evangelicals or good samaritans, but to me they were angels. They helped me at one of the lowest points of my life, and asked for nothing in return.

Once I was back on I-90, I got a ride from a female trucker going all the way to Pennsylvania. It felt like a miracle. As it got dark, she said, "Don't get the wrong idea here, but I don't like to sleep in the truck so I'm planning on getting a hotel room. You're welcome to stay in my room," she paused, looked directly at me, "but it's *just* to sleep." As I took in her three-hundred-plus pound frame, tattoos and facial hair, I quickly assured her that "just sleep" was good with me. I made it to Boston by nightfall the next day.

When I set out on my quixotic, thirteen-hundred-mile journey I didn't know what to expect, but I ended up finding one of life's greatest gifts: kindness. At a time when I was broken and lost, strangers opened up their cars, hearts and wallets to me. And remarkably, by picking up a sketchy stranger on the side of the road, they did it at great personal risk.

They taught me that kindness is doing something for someone with no expectation or even possibility of receiving anything in return. The most meaningful things I've ever done in my life have been when I least expected any return, which ironically ends up being more rewarding than I could ever imagine.

Hitchhiking as a form of transportation is long since gone, but the spirit of their kindness lives on in me. It's a gift that reminds me what the human experience really means—to serve each other without regard for self. It's a gift that uplifts and inspires me to keep repaying for the rest of my brief stay on this earth.

The morning of departure
Minneapolis, Minnesota–May 1979

(Not so) Great Expectations

All external expectations ... just fall away in the face
of death, leaving only what is truly important.
—STEVE JOBS

———❈———

DURING THE SUMMER following my first year at Hobart College, I received a letter from the dean of students informing me that I had to take a year off from school because I failed three of my courses. I was upset, but also offended. To fail implies that I tried; for at least one of the courses in question, I never even went to class. That said, in just over one year's time, I had been expelled from high school and suspended from college. I needed a change of plan.

What I really needed was a serious kick in the butt, but I didn't have the wherewithal or physical mechanics to do it to myself, so I decided to join one of the best butt-kicking organizations in the world: the United States Marine Corps. When I told my friends of my intentions at a party later that night, they laughed. I bet each one of them $50 that I would enlist the next day.

As I drove down to the Marine Corps recruiting office early the next morning, I thought about the stories I heard of recruits drowning in the swamps or dying of heat exhaustion at Parris Island due to brutal training practices. I didn't know how credible those were, but even the thought of being eaten alive by sand fleas with a psychotic drill instructor screaming in my face was stressing me out.

I didn't want to come across as a wimp, so I casually asked the marine sergeant if there were options other than Parris Island. "Absolutely!" he replied enthusiastically. "It used to be that you were assigned to either PI or San Diego depending on which side of the Mississippi you lived in, but they just changed that. Do you want to go to San Diego?"

San Diego? Are you kidding me? I thought. *How hard could that be?* I was elated. I even went so far as to envision staying out there after boot camp, spending a few weeks at the beach, living the dream. "Oh yeah, I definitely want to go to San Diego," I said. He said that all I needed to do was assure him I wasn't a criminal, drug user or a homosexual and he would take care of everything. Now it was time to collect money from my faithless friends.

In the early morning hours of September 18, 1980, I arrived at the processing station in Boston, Massachusetts to receive my final orders before taking a government shuttle to the airport. As I read through my documents I came to a page with my flight itinerary that had me leaving Boston and arriving in Charleston, South Carolina. There was obviously some kind of mistake.

I approached the desk sergeant as I would a travel agent who had mixed-up my reservations. "Excuse me, but there's an error in my reservations. It says I'm going to Charleston, South Carolina, but I'm supposed to be going to San Diego." He barely glanced at it and said there was no mistake.

"I'm sorry," I said politely, "but my recruiter assured me that I was going to San Diego, perhaps we can call him and get this straightened out."

"Shut up!" he screamed. "Shut your nasty, maggot mouth! You belong to the United States Marine Corps and you will go where we tell you to go. And you're going to Parris Island. Now go sit down over there and I don't want to hear one more word out of you."

Like a fighter who just took a flurry of blows to the head at the end of a round, I stumbled back to the bench. For the first time it hit me what I had gotten myself into. I *belonged* to the Marine Corps. I had signed away my rights and my freedom, and there was absolutely nothing I could do about it. I was going to Parris Island.

Feelings of shock, anger, denial, and depression were bouncing around inside my head like a pin ball machine. But most of all I was terrified. My trip down to South Carolina felt like Marlow's journey in Conrad's *Heart of Darkness*—heading into the unknown, consumed with apprehension, foreboding, and fear.

My experience at Parris Island, of course, didn't turn out to be anything like what I had imagined. The moment we arrived to the sound of screaming drill instructors telling us to get off the bus— and for the next three months—the reality of the actual experience replaced the images my fear had created.

I later realized that my problem had nothing to do with the change of orders from San Diego to Parris Island—my problem was the perception I had of both places. I had a picture in my mind of Parris Island as a place of terror and San Diego as easy street—and both were wrong. My drill instructors weren't "psychotic" (although there were times it seemed that way) and the training in San Diego isn't any easier than Parris Island.

There have been many times when I've expected things to be a certain way only to be disappointed when they didn't go as I'd hoped. It took a long time for me to understand this, but whenever I have expectations like that it's almost impossible for things to go the way I want because so much of what happens is out of my control.

In fact, having set expectations is a sure formula for perpetual disappointment.

I was mentally and emotionally set on San Diego, but Parris Island proved to be one of the most invaluable experiences of my life, which is why I'm careful to avoid having expectations of anything.

I can't accept life as it is when I'm holding onto a picture of what I wanted it to be.

The greatest expectation, I've found, is to not have any expectations at all.

Official Marine photo
Parris Island, South Carolina–December 1980

Contents Under Pressure

Circumstance does not make the man; it reveals him to himself.
—JAMES ALLEN

⊶ ⊷

BEFORE LEAVING FOR Marine Corps boot camp, a friend who was a former marine gave me this advice: "Artie, when they ask for volunteers, it's never for anything good. Whatever you do, *never* volunteer. The best strategy is to be as anonymous as possible. If they don't know your name, that's a really good thing." So that was my plan, to live in the shadows for three months. It would prove to be a short-lived strategy.

On the first night, we were in the barracks standing at attention when Sergeant Roberts, our toughest, scariest drill instructor, shouted: "Any privates who have spent time in college step forward, now!" No one, including me, moved. "I've seen your files and I know at least one of you nasty little maggots has had some college so I better see somebody step up right now." *Damn*, I thought, *I am so screwed.* I took a deep breath and a step forward.

Roberts went ballistic. He stormed down the squad bay, put his blood-red face one inch from mine, and unleashed a full-throated verbal assault so vitriolic I thought he was going to have a heart attack. "When I asked for recruits with college experience, you just stood there Private Dwight! You are a liar and a cheat and a disgrace to the Marine Corps. You make me sick! I am going to destroy you. Do we understand each other?!" It was a long time ago, and my memory is a bit fuzzy, but it's possible I wet my pants just a little bit.

From that moment until the end of basic training, Sergeant Roberts inflicted unrelenting pressure on me. I was a human bulls-eye for his rage and disdain. Whether it was drills, inspections or rifle cleaning, everything I did was wrong. I was singled out as the worst example of a marine. Whenever I allegedly messed up, he frequently forced the entire platoon to get down in the sand pit with me for correctional exercise—a tactic intended to ratchet up the pressure by turning my fellow recruits against me. It was effective.

He gave me additional duties that included extra night fire-watch shifts, which meant I had to go with less sleep, adding to the intense stress and pressure I was experiencing. A few times he called me into his office and shut the blinds. "Have I ever hit you Dwight?"

"Sir, no sir!"

He punched me in the stomach. "That's good, because we're not allowed to touch recruits. So you're certain I've never hit you, right, Dwight?"

"Sir, no sir!" And then he punched me again, harder.

After we were trained in pugil sticks, large poles padded at each end designed to simulate rifles and bayonets, recruits faced off against each other in simulated combat. Sergeant Roberts called me out first to fight one of the biggest men in our platoon. When the whistle blew, I hit him as hard and fast as I could. When the referee declared me the winner, I was as surprised as everyone else.

But Roberts looked furious. When the referee signaled for two new fighters, he shouted with a sneer, "Not you, Dwight. You stay in there!" And he sent in another big recruit to face me. Somehow I found the strength and adrenaline I needed and won that fight too. My platoon cheered wildly for me.

Roberts shouted again, "Stay in there, Dwight!" The cheering stopped. Even the referee looked stunned, but he wasn't about to overrule another drill instructor in front of recruits. He ordered two men into the ring to fight me at once. I barely had enough strength left to lift my stick in defense. They hit me hard, fast and often until I collapsed into the sand.

As my fellow recruits helped me out of the ring, something profound had changed for me, my platoon and even Sergeant Roberts. I had taken his best shots and refused to quit. In full view of eighty men, I showed him something that he didn't expect to see; I was a fighter.

On that day, I earned the respect of my fellow recruits, and I think Sergeant Roberts', too. He kept the pressure on me until graduation, but the intensity and maliciousness behind it was gone. He never said it, but I suspect I passed the test. I even earned a meritorious promotion to private first class at graduation.

It's a misperception that military training is intended to "break" people. Roberts wasn't trying to break me—he was trying to *expose* me. It was his job to identify the recruits who might falter under the stress of combat, and make mistakes that could kill their fellow marines. The time to reveal those flaws is during training, because it's too late once the bullets start flying. He was doing his job, and I honor and respect him for it.

This experience taught me that pressure is what reveals my true character—it exposes the flaws so I can correct them and grow stronger. Difficult, stressful and challenging circumstances are necessary to test my progress and show me where I need to change. I don't learn anything about myself when everything is going well—it's only under pressure that I can discover who I really am.

When an orange is squeezed (a.k.a. put under pressure), the only thing that comes out is orange juice because that's all that it has inside it—it is pure, whole and complete. In the same way, if I have true integrity and I am put under pressure, then the only possible response

I can make is to think and act with integrity. The degree of pressure doesn't matter—either I have integrity or I don't.

I work hard to strengthen my character during the easier, uneventful periods of my life so I'm better prepared for the challenges when they arise. And when I'm feeling squeezed by life's challenges I say to myself, "Bring it on. Squeeze away. Let's find out what I'm really made of."

At the confidence course on graduation day
Parris Island, South Carolina–December 1980

Look at This

An unexamined life is not worth living.
—SOCRATES

I N MY THIRD YEAR at Hobart College I was living proof that Darwin was wrong; the human species is not evolving. I was cocky and confident on the surface, but that was merely a facade shielding a warehouse of insecurities. I was in English Literature with Andrew Harvey, an Oxford-educated professor who taught with a passion, turbulence, brilliance and intensity that simultaneously inspired and terrified me.

A physically small man with wiry, disheveled hair, he would burst into the room like an intellectual tornado, stirring up my thoughts and emotions, forcing me to reevaluate everything I thought I knew about life or myself. I was always careful to avoid his omniscient, feral eyes, fearing he could see through my act, or worse, that he might call on me as I likely had not read the previous night's assignment. There was no way to fake it with this guy and I had sense enough to know it.

As class was ending one day, he said, "Mr. Dwight, I'd like to see you after class." In two months, no one had *ever* been asked to stay after class. I was the first.

Paralyzed with apprehension as my classmates filed out of the room, my good friend John DeRosa stayed as long as he could. He took his time gathering up his books and whispered into my ear as he left, "Good luck," which really meant, *you are so screwed and thank God it's not me.*

When the door closed behind John, Professor Harvey wasted no time with small talk. "Mr. Dwight," he said, "when I first met you I thought you were quite sure of yourself, but now I don't think that at all. I think you're neurotic and don't have the slightest idea of what you're doing."

As I struggled to absorb the force of this verbal nuke, he continued, "If you don't find the philosophical basis for your existence by the time you are twenty-one you might as well kill yourself." Exact quote. His words crushed me like a three-hundred-pound man jumping on a cheap card table. When someone summarizes your life in a few sentences, and exposes you for the fraud that you are, you tend to remember it.

The truth is that I didn't change much that year or even in the next two years, but his words stayed with me. They pierced my defenses and grew like spiritual seeds in my heart. I couldn't shake their truth. He was right. I was wasting my life. He called me to make a change that eventually happened—a change that transformed my life in every way.

Socrates said that "an unexamined life is not worth living." In a blunt, brutal way Andrew Harvey challenged me to examine my life. I think he knew that a subtle approach was not going to work. He was right. I needed a shotgun blast and I got it because there was a lot at stake. A wasted life, by choice, is a tragedy.

I've learned that every moment contains an opportunity to learn, change, or grow—to elevate myself physically, mentally, emotionally, or spiritually. Sometimes it's a steady, persistent knocking and other times it's a blinking sign with an arrow saying, "You need to *look at this,* Art!" Sometimes I actually hear those words coming from this beautiful, intelligent woman, who looks an awful lot like my wife.

It never feels good to get those signals and realize that I'm responsible for whatever it is I'm trying to avoid—so my first instinct is to push back. The temptation to blame, excuse, justify, deny or evade is almost overpowering. And yet this is where the battle begins. If I have the courage to drop my defenses and take an honest *look at myself*—it is the first step to new insight and a new life.

Accepting that the only place to look for answers is within me is never easy or pleasant. But no matter what kind of mental or emotional gymnastics I use to try and get out of it, I can't alter or change the truth that the path always leads back to me. This process is still hard for me, but I have made progress in recognizing my part sooner.

Now, I see every day as a new beginning, filled with a fresh slate of moments to help me improve my life and the lives of others. I feel so blessed to have these opportunities because, like the prodigal son, I know what it feels like to be completely lost. The view from the top of the mountain is even more spectacular when you've spent a long time at the bottom.

Andrew Harvey challenged me to find the "philosophical basis for my existence." At the time, I had no idea what he was talking about. I think (and hope) I do now. I'm here to do exactly what I'm doing now; sharing the moments and insights of my life that I hope will inspire others to do the same. I believe that self-examination and expression can change the world, but I also know that the only measurement of this is through action.

In that regard, Andrew Harvey is quite a role model. He has written more than thirty books and is one of the world's foremost experts on spiritual transformation. I feel lucky that our life's paths intersected and will always be grateful to him for taking an interest in me and giving me a hard dose of truth that I desperately needed to hear. He helped give me new life and I intend to make the most of it.

Andrew Harvey
Photo: David Sutton Studios

Father Knows Best

When I was a boy of fourteen, my father was so ignorant I could hardly
stand to have the old man around. But when I got to be twenty-one,
I was astonished at how much the old man had learned in seven years.
—MARK TWAIN

❦

I FEEL SO CONTENT TODAY that I sometimes wonder if the first half of my life, with all the pain, drama and chaos, even happened at all. But whenever I get too comfortable, something from my past invariably surfaces to disabuse me, like the phone call I got from an old Deerfield Academy friend, Bob "Hoss" Friedman. "Art, when you were at Deerfield, you were messed up. I mean, you were *seriously, seriously* messed up. How did you get your life together?"

There were so many twists and turns, successes and setbacks in my journey that there was no simple answer to this question, but there was one defining moment that marked the end of my self-destructive ways and the beginning of a new life. This change started when I woke up with my face in a gutter outside a bar in a seedy section of Hartford, Connecticut.

After graduating Hobart College in 1983, I moved to Pennsylvania to be with my girlfriend. Six months later, she met a successful businessman and dropped me like a hot potato, leaving me to wonder exactly what it was I was doing with my life. I was waiting tables at night, sleeping past noon and I had no purpose or direction beyond that.

Depressed and discouraged, I turned to alcohol and drugs. That wasn't enough so I packed up my life's possessions into my car and headed north on I-95 for a change of scenery. I met up with friends in New York where we partied non-stop for days. My time there was a blur, but when one of my friends said to me, "Art, you do know college is over, right?" I was conscious enough to know that I had worn out my welcome.

I continued my journey north, went out drinking with an old friend near Hartford and somehow ended up at his ex-girlfriend's apartment. Around four in the morning, her counsel wasn't as subtle as my New York friend's had been: "You can't stay here." I may have been a pathetic drunk, but I could still take a hint. I stumbled out of her apartment and eventually found myself alone at a bar in Hartford drinking a long-neck Budweiser at seven in the morning.

A sketchy-looking guy entered the bar and asked if I would buy him a drink. Just as the bartender was about to throw him out, I nodded to the seat next to me and bought the man a beer. The bartender didn't look happy, but I was buying so there was nothing he could do about it. We eventually left the bar together. In an alley with some of his homeless friends who seemed to appear out of nowhere, I continued to drink myself senseless.

I didn't have a frame of reference to know I had hit rock bottom, but I'm reasonably sure that drinking with homeless people in an alley was it. According to the law of attraction, I don't attract what I *want* in life, I attract what I *am*. And at that moment in my life, I believed I was worthless, undeserving, and unlovable.

But in a strange way I felt relieved because I knew that my free-fall had to be over. As I looked at my new companions, I realized that I was no longer in the *process* of losing it. I had lost it. I had to decide if this was the life I wanted.

I couldn't do this anymore. I needed help.

I thought of the one person who always helped me when I needed it. My father. As I drove to his house I felt so ashamed that I almost turned around, but like *An Officer and a Gentleman's* Zach Mayo, I had nowhere else to go. If he didn't take me in, I didn't know what I would do. When my father opened the door, I just stood there. I was too burned-out to speak. My dad later recalled that I didn't need to say anything. Everything about me screamed *Help me*. And that's what he did.

It was obvious that my way wasn't working out so well, so I decided to give his way a try. Over the next several months I healed up while my dad helped me with my job search. We agreed that advertising sales was the best fit and he went to work setting up interviews all over New England for me—a process that led to a twenty-year career in the newspaper business.

In retrospect, it's no accident that my father was the one I turned to when all seemed lost. Although my father's life in politics allowed little time for us together when I was growing up, one thing I could always count on is that he would help me when I asked for it. His support was priceless, but the greatest gift my father gave me were the principles he lived his life by.

He was the master of the maxim. Whenever I screwed up, he'd share an adage that fit the crime so perfectly it was like a nuclear bomb that wiped out any hope that he might actually buy the arguments, excuses or explanations I worked so hard to create. Here's a sample of some of his favorites:

- Two wrongs don't make a right.
- Don't judge another until you walk a mile in their shoes.
- It doesn't matter what someone else does, it only matters what you do.
- Oh, what a tangled web we weave, when at first we practice to deceive.

At their core, his principles were based on one absolute, irrefutable truth: I am responsible for my behavior. He taught me how to act with integrity and to *never* justify my behavior because of the behavior of others; which obliterated my twisted logic that if someone else was doing it, it must be okay.

During my profligate youth I failed to heed his counsel, but I couldn't escape it. I once saw a t-shirt that said, "I used to be schizophrenic, but we're okay now." It's funny, sure, but that's exactly how it feels to me when I hear my father's voice in my head. And when I came to the crossroads of my life that morning in Hartford, the message he planted in my brain was that if my actions got me into that mess, then my actions could get me out of it.

Years later I re-read the Bible's story of the prodigal son who ends up starving and alone after squandering his inheritance. At his darkest hour he decides to return home to beg his father to hire him as a common laborer. He returns believing that he deserves to be shunned, but when his father sees him, he rejoices and orders a great feast to celebrate because what was lost has now been found.

Two thousand years later another prodigal son found his way back home. Despite all of my failures and self-destructive behavior, my father never gave up me. While it's true that my decisions and actions turned my life around, I don't think that would have been possible without my father's wisdom, which did more than just guide me, it saved me.

Don Dwight
Lyme, New Hampshire–March 2010

A (Not So) Humble Paperboy

If only I had humility, I'd be perfect.
—TED TURNER

EARLY IN MY CAREER, anxious to put the pain, guilt and regret of my youth behind me, I felt compelled to succeed and make something of my life. To me, I'd find redemption in achievement, titles, position and money. Within minutes of receiving a promotion to my first significant management job at the *Concord Monitor* newspaper, I drove out to the local mall, picked out the biggest nameplate I could find, and had it engraved with my name and title.

I took one look at it and said to myself, *Oh yeah, I am the man. Chicks are going to love this.*

Call me superficial, narcissistic, sad, but I loved that nameplate. I wasn't just a manager—I was a *director*—and I wanted everyone who walked into my office to know it. But as great as I thought my title was, the reality of being a circulation director of a small newspaper is a tough, humbling job. There are times when the turnover of carrier routes is so high that everyone in the department, including me, had to deliver newspapers.

I wouldn't admit this at the time, but I enjoyed delivering newspapers. Like mowing the lawn, it had a definite beginning and end.

It felt good to get a break from the stress of management and perform simple, satisfying work. I also loved seeing how happy our customers were to get their afternoon paper. It was a nice reminder of the true purpose of our business.

One cold, gray, winter afternoon, with two bags bulging with papers slung over my shoulders, dispensing the news door-to-door, I saw a young woman walking toward me who I recognized, but simultaneously thought, *It's just not possible. This is New Hampshire, America's Siberia. No one from Main Line Philadelphia just "shows up" here. This cannot be happening.*

But as she got closer, there was no doubt it was Eveline, the sister of my college girlfriend, Denise. This was my personal "Nightmare on School Street" starring Eveline as Freddy Kreuger. I considered running in the other direction, but I was reasonably sure she already recognized me, too. I could hear that night's call to her sister as if it were already a memory:

"Hey Denise," Eveline says. "Guess who I ran into? Art Dwight. And you'll never guess what he's doing. He's a paperboy!"

"Shut up, Eveline, you're not serious!"

"No, it's true. What a loser!"

Earlier that day, I was a self-assured circulation director. Now, I was a college-educated paperboy. Life can be cruel, but only because I decided it was. The truth is that my paperboy drama was *entirely* self-created. The only problem was my own insecurity. I wanted Denise to believe that I was a big success, or for her to regret breaking up with me, even though it was arguably one of her better decisions.

What I needed, but didn't have, was humility, which to me is one of the highest and noblest of all character traits. Humility is the opposite of everything I was focused on such as money, achievement or what people thought of me. Indeed, if I had been humble, none of that would have mattered.

At the time, I believed that delivering newspapers was something that was beneath me. I was carefully building an image of myself as a person on the rise—and the higher I went—the better I was. I've since reversed that belief. To deliver newspapers or perform any act of service is the true path to becoming "somebody." To rise high means going low. The servant among us truly is the greatest.

In the past, I tried to hide my weaknesses, failures or mistakes with the intent of making a favorable impression on others. Yet when the truth came out, as it always did, the only impression I created is that I was inauthentic. I've since learned that to be humble means that I'm willing to be vulnerable and share the things I fear the most. And ironically, that leads to true invulnerability.

The more I learn about humility, I realize just how much further I have to go. But instead of being discouraged, I'm inspired because this quest brings out the best in me. I will always be human and flawed, but pursuing humility is one of the most exciting, gratifying, and fulfilling journeys of my life.

Running an Easter egg hunt for news carriers
Concord, New Hampshire-April 1995

Special Delivery

We make a living by what we get, but we make a life by what we give.
—SIR WINSTON CHURCHILL

WHEN I WAS A BOY I had a limited view of heroism. My heroes were powerful, fearless, and flawless men. To put this into context, President Richard Nixon was one of my heroes, which may have explained why my sisters' Dory and Ellie routinely called me a "male chauvinist pig" and "junior hard-hat, red neck."

During my time as a circulation director, I had an opportunity to see heroism in an entirely different way, starting with the obvious truth that women can be heroes too. One woman in particular taught me that heroism is more about quietly devoting your life to serving others than rescuing damsels in distress.

When I took charge of the circulation department in 1991, Ernestine "Ernie" Gay had already been delivering newspapers every afternoon for thirty-nine years. To the customers she faithfully served in New London, New Hampshire, she was much more than a newspaper carrier—she was an integral part of the fabric of their community and their link to the world. They depended on her deliveries, which were as timely and reliable as a Swiss watch.

During my fourth year at the paper, our management team decided to make some big changes by converting from afternoon to morning delivery and adding a Sunday newspaper six months after that. For the nearly three hundred adult and youth newspaper carriers, this meant they would have to deliver papers between one and six a.m., seven days a week. This switch was so extreme that other newspapers reported turning over the entire delivery force.

During a route-by-route assessment of delivery agents we could lose with this change, I moved one name to the top of the list. Ernie Gay. At her age, I didn't think there was any way she would, or could, continue delivering in the middle of the night, seven days a week, but she deserved to hear about this change directly from me. We had never met before because she lived forty miles from our office and received her papers via bulk delivery. It was time to meet the legend.

As we sat down in her living room, I knew my first impressions of Ernie Gay would be the same if I had known her for a lifetime. Her character and the values she lives her life by are as strong as the granite for which New Hampshire is famous. She is a living icon to the protestant work ethic, a tough Yankee who endures any hardship, possesses uncommon dedication, and never makes excuses for herself.

Before I could say anything, Ernie jumped right in to tell me everything we were doing wrong in the circulation department. Trying not to feel defensive, I quickly realized her concerns weren't for herself—they were about her customers. She was especially upset about the "cheap" plastic bags (which I ordered to save money). In wet weather, she said she would have to use three bags, plus rubber bands to make sure her customers received a dry, undamaged paper.

When Ernie finished, she finally gave me the opening to share the reason for my visit. I informed her of the upcoming changes and asked her if she intended to stay on. She looked at me like I was insane. "Stay on?" she said, her eyes suddenly wet and her voice rippling with emotion, "Of course I'm going to stay on. I've been taking care of my customers since Dwight Eisenhower was president. I could never leave them."

To put what Ernie said into context, she had been delivering newspapers every day except Sunday since 1952. When the paper added Sunday delivery, she served 250 customers every day for ten more years. In total, over fifty-four years (approximately 16,500 days) she made four million deliveries and drove more than a million miles, in every type of weather, including sub-zero temperatures, massive snow and ice storms, and on unpaved, muddy roads.

Ernie never once asked the newspaper for help or missed a day due to illness or other reasons. She saw it as her responsibility and she never once let her customers down. The bottom line was that nothing stopped Ernie from doing her job. With all due respect to Cal "Iron Man" Ripken, his 2,632 consecutive games record looks pretty thin compared to Ernie's achievement.

To this day Ernie inspires me far more than the heroes of my youth. Ernie's selfless dedication and uncommon devotion to her customers are what legends are made of. Ernie's son told me that as she got older he urged her to give up the route, but of course she would have none of that. To Ernie, delivering newspapers was more than a contract; it was a covenant, an unbreakable commitment. It was a promise to deliver the news every day and nothing was going to prevent her from fulfilling it, including weather, exhaustion, or illness.

Ernie still lives in those beautiful New London hills, but her time as a newspaper carrier came to an end in 2006. And even then it wasn't by choice. If it weren't for state vision standards, she told me she'd still be out there delivering every day, just like she did, for fifty-four years.

Ernestine "Ernie" Gay
New London, New Hampshire–May 2005

Free Falling

Fear knocked on the door, faith opened it,
and lo, there was no one there.
—OLD IRISH PROVERB

———

ONE OF MY GREATEST JOYS is hiking in the mountains. I love the sound of running streams, wildlife thrashing through the bushes, sunlight dappling off the leaves and especially the easy peace of the forest. Climbing to the summit, I feel increasingly joyful and fully alive—the closest thing to heaven on earth. And then…as I arrive at the top of the mountain…I freak out. Every time. It's a buzz kill.

Acrophobia is described as an "extreme and irrational fear of heights." I didn't mind the diagnosis, but for someone who prides himself on personal change, I had had enough. It was time to do something about it. I read something by Vic Johnson that grabbed me: "If I fear it, I must do it." He said that we cannot grow unless we are willing to take action despite our fears. That was *exactly* what I was looking for.

I took a big gulp of Vic's *Kool-Aid*, called a sky diving organization and booked a jump for the following Saturday. I called out my acrophobia like he was a separate person. *Yeah, I'm going sky diving*, I told him, *and you're coming with me. What do you think of that? You're not so tough now, are you?*

On dive day, I was still feeling good after the pre-dive training, except for one ominous moment when the instructor stood at the opening of a mock airplane and said, "Now, about this time, you'll be looking down from fifteen thousand feet, your knees will buckle, and some of you will start screaming 'No! No! No!' but with all that wind up there, it sounds to us like 'Go! Go! Go!'"

When it came time to board the plane, anxious to get this over with as quickly as possible, I rudely pushed my way to the front of the line. If I hadn't been so fixated on going first, I might have taken a moment to think and realize that planes load back-to-front, which meant, of course, that I would now jump last. *Kill me now.*

Once we were airborne, my instructor sat behind me and strapped himself to me in preparation for the jump. I was already far enough outside my comfort zone, but the experience of having a stranger strapped onto me from behind without a millimeter of separation took it to a new level. And as if this wasn't enough of a boundary violation, my adrenaline-junkie instructor started cracking jokes about how this was his first jump and how he wished he hadn't had so many beers this morning because he thought he might pass out.

When we hit the jump zone, one-by-one the other jumpers leapt out of the plane. As I watched each person disappear into the abyss, I desperately fought to control the fear that was consuming me. Finally, we shuffled like crabs to the open doorway where I got my first look at the ground from fifteen thousand feet, a sight that obliterated my last vestige of courage. I could hear my fear mocking me. *So who's the tough guy now?*

Just as we were about to jump, the pilot shouted from the front of the plane, "We've overshot the drop zone. We've got to circle around again." This unwelcome stay of execution was surely my karmic penalty for pushing my way to the front of the line. The good news was that after ten more minutes of staring at the ground and hyperventilating in the cold, thin November air, I wasn't scared anymore. I was catatonic.

When we got the green light to jump, my instructor pushed us out of the plane and into our free fall. I was supposed to watch my altimeter and pull the ripcord at ten thousand feet. I didn't check any-thing. I was too preoccupied with falling to my death at two hundred feet per second. My instructor screamed into my ear loudly enough to cut through the cacophony of wind, "Did you pull the cord?!!"

"NO!" I screamed back.

"Then we're really screwed," he shouted, which pierced my cata-tonia just enough for me to realize I really was going to die.

A moment later, he waved the rip cord handle in front of my face. "I was just messing with you," he said, and laughed like it was the funniest thing he ever heard in his life. The chute had already deployed and I didn't even know it. We descended slowly for the next ten minutes until finally, mercifully, we hit the ground. Unlike some of the other jumpers who were hugging, high-fiving each other and screaming about how it was the greatest rush of their lives, I wasn't happy or even relieved. I was fried.

Interestingly, the quest to conquer my fear of heights led to a more important discovery. I realized that the most courageous thing I've ever done wasn't jumping out of that plane. It was *admitting* that I was scared to do it. And that the most significant breakthroughs of my life all started with one simple admission, "I'm scared."

Trying to deny, cover up, or run around my fears causes more problems for me than the fear itself. For most of my life, my problem wasn't that I was scared; it's that I was scared to say I was scared. If I didn't do something because I was afraid, I did everything I could to hide the underlying reason.

Considering I had so many fears such as heights, rejection, public speaking, poverty, sickness, obesity, criticism, abandonment, and of course, death, I was doing a lot of covering up! I could see how my efforts to hide my fears could cause other people to perceive me as inauthentic, or worse, dishonest.

When I finally learned to get out of my own way and say that I was scared, it wiped out suspicion and created space for trust to grow. When I open up my heart and allow myself to be vulnerable, it strips away the superficial garbage that so often gets in the way of relationships. And when I'm honest—it gives the other person the emotional safety to be honest, too—and that's when the magic in relationships begin.

I've learned to develop the habit of taking an honest inventory of my feelings and sharing what's really going on with me. I've found that every time I admit my fear, my fear grows weaker and I grow stronger. As my fears lose their power over me, I'm able to take my life back and start living as Thoreau put it, "the life that I had imagined."

It's also a lot safer (and saner) than jumping out of airplanes.

Finishing Strong

I run because it's so symbolic of life. You have to drive yourself to overcome the obstacles. You might feel that you can't, but then you find your inner strength and realize you are capable of so much more.

—ARTHUR BLANK

◦—◦ ≍╪≍ ◦—◦

THE YEAR I TURNED FORTY I decided to mark the occasion by running my first marathon. This was a surprising choice considering I thought that anyone who runs 26.2 miles was either suicidal or insane. Clearly it would be physically impossible for me to do it. So I set out to do the impossible, testing my theories on the psychological mindset of marathoners in the process.

After six months of training, race day finally arrived; a cloudless, sunny and unusually hot October day in Washington, DC. Veteran marathoners know that hot and sunny is a brutal combination that can neutralize the best training regimen. As a blissfully ignorant novice, I thought the weather was ideal. In a few short hours, my assessment of the conditions would be recalibrated.

On the advice of Lisa "LG" Levy, a friend and experienced marathoner, I put my name on my shirt with fabric ink so the crowd could offer personal encouragement. In big red and blue letters I emblazoned "Super Art" on my chest. It was both the smartest and dumbest thing I would do that day.

When the gun went off, nerves, excitement, and adrenaline fueled an extremely fast start. Hitting sub-seven minute miles (more than a minute faster than my training pace) I turned the corner onto M Street in Georgetown, the crowd was jacked up; people were screaming, "Art! Art! Go, Super Art!" I started pointing to the crowd, high-fiving kids, scanning the field thinking, *maybe I could win this thing.* I was superhuman. I *was* Super Art. I was delusional.

I continued my blistering pace down Constitution Avenue where my daughters were holding "Go Daddy" signs. By the time I got to the other side of the mall approaching mile thirteen, suddenly Super Art wasn't feeling so super. My fantasy of winning the race evaporated as quickly as my adrenaline.

The race then went out to Haines Point, which is a long, lonely, crowdless six-mile stretch—a graveyard for the dreams of many thousands of marathoners before me. It was here that I earned my Ph.D in the meaning of the runner's expression *hitting the wall.* When you hit the wall, everything ends in an instant; adrenaline, willpower, motivation, and physical strength.

The sun and heat conspired to suck the life out of me. I was severely dehydrated—like an engine that runs out of oil, my body seized up and almost ceased functioning. My legs were so badly cramped I could barely move. But it was here that I discovered my ability to find strength that defies physiological explanation.

With my body screaming, *For God's sake, stop,* I confirmed that my original hypothesis was correct, marathoners *are* insane. But one thought broke through the pain: *I must finish this race.* Somehow I willed myself to continue—every painful step felt like I was pushing through wet cement. When I crossed the Fourteenth Street Bridge around mile twenty, the full force of the midday sun was bearing down as the mercury rose into the high seventies.

At mile twenty-three, the violent battle between my body and mind had reached its apex; my body was finished. I had nothing left. But just as I was resigned to do the unthinkable, to quit, I heard cheering from the top of a bridge near Arlington Cemetery. I looked up and saw this sign, PAIN IS TEMPORARY, BUT GLORY LASTS FOREVER. The truth of those words exploded in my mind. I realized that my pain exists *only* in this moment, but the glory of finishing this race, today, will stay with me for the rest of my life.

Like Popeye who just downed a fresh can of spinach, those words gave me new life. Any thought of quitting was gone and I started *running* again, certain I would finish. As I climbed the spiraling rise toward the Marine Corps Memorial, the crowd was electric and the cheers for "Super Art" filled the air again like I was some kind of rock star.

I like to pride myself on eschewing ego, but I'll admit it, it was pretty cool. It fueled my drive to the finish line, which I crossed three hours and forty-two minutes after I started.

I found that marathons are a metaphor for life. The training a time of growth; the miles in Georgetown were the reward of that labor; the cheers of the crowd and especially my family, were a time of celebration; Haines Point was a period of suffering where I learned what I was really made of. And then the finish line—an achievement of a worthy goal, but not for the race itself, but for who I became in the process of finishing it.

I learned a lot about myself that day, but above all I discovered an inexhaustible will that is far stronger than my body, my thoughts, or emotions. When reason or my body tells me I'm done, I know I can always find something more to take me as far as I need to go. There is always a way to overcome seemingly insurmountable obstacles.

Crossing the finish line, Marine Corps Marathon
Washington, DC–October 2000

This is the Moment

It doesn't get any better than this.
—Michael J. Simon

I WISH I HAD made that phone call.

I thought about it often enough. But as the years rolled by it became harder to do. Where do you start? What do you say? How do you reconnect with a friend you haven't talked to in years? So I never made that call. I'd give anything to make it now, but I had no way to know that I'd never get the chance.

On September 11, 2001, one of my closest college friends was killed when the first plane hit the World Trade Center. Mike Simon and I had not spoken in sixteen years. At his funeral service, attended by more than one thousand people, I was shocked to learn that Mike had lost both of his parents and I didn't even know.

Mike was my partner in crime, literally. We arrived early senior year to take possession of the Red House, an off-campus residence with a reputation so lurid that to this day I only talk about it with my former housemates. It was missing a few essentials, namely furniture. After a few beers, we raided the dorms and loaded up my car with as much furniture as we could stuff into it.

We were driving back around two a.m. when a black sedan started tailgating me. I took random turns to shake him, but he stayed right on my tail. Thinking some townies were messing with us, I turned to Mike and asked him what he thought. He gave me a big, goofy grin and yelled, "Let's punch it!" I did.

There's nothing like putting the pedal-to-the-metal on a manual shift, four-cylinder Toyota Corolla. Going eighty-miles-per-hour on a dark, narrow back road was the rush of a lifetime. Fueled by beer and adrenaline, Mike and I were living the alpha male dream. We had no fear, no worries, and absolutely no common sense.

We were unstoppable—at least until I turned a corner and saw three police cars blocking the road with lights flashing. Any hope that this was just a late-night coffee and donuts party for the Geneva Police Department vanished the moment the black sedan that had been following me flipped on his flashing lights.

I was ordered to get out of the car and get face down on the road. They told me to recite the alphabet backward, which I don't think I could do today sober. When I got stuck on Z, I was taken into the station, photographed, finger printed and put into a cell. I was charged with DUI and nine other moving violations, including running two red lights, three stop signs and going eighty mph in a thirty mph zone, which was apparently a felony.

I eventually pleaded guilty to one misdemeanor and my arrest was expunged (until now), but the inside joke that Mike and I shared was that they never questioned the purloined furniture—something that surely would have resulted in our dismissal from college because of our prior record in the dean's office. It had been a few years, but it was pretty bad and we didn't think they had forgotten about it.

I'd like nothing more than to reminisce and laugh about this with Mike today. In the months following his death, I struggled to make sense of it. I felt confused, guilty and angry. I had dreams about personally killing Osama Bin Laden. I even contacted the Army about reinstating my commission. They were polite enough, but basically said, "Thanks for the offer old man, but we think we can handle it."

I got another shock a few months later when I learned that one of my closest grade-school friends, David Rivers, was also killed that day. He was attending a trade show on the top floor of the first tower at the Windows to the World restaurant. I read a newspaper article that said his five-year-old son asked his mother at David's service, "Why did Daddy have to be there that day?"

I was struggling with that same question when I remembered something that Mike Simon said to me many years earlier. We were driving down the New York State Thruway late one night when he got extremely excited and shouted out, "You know, Art, it doesn't get any better than this!"

"What do you mean?" I asked.

"I mean, this moment, right now, driving down the highway, drinking beer with you, is the best! It doesn't get any better than this!"

At the time, I thought Mike was babbling and I didn't really get it. But I think I do now. What he was sharing was the wisdom of the ages, one of the most profound truths of all—that the only thing that exists is the moment I have *right now*. There is no other moment. The past is gone and the future hasn't happened. The only thing that counts is what I do with my life in *this moment*. And that's exactly how Mike lived his life—with enthusiasm, passion and inexhaustible energy.

His words inspired me to make changes in my life that I've kept to this day. I saw that the regret and guilt of not calling him was keeping me chained to the past. I can't live in the past and be present at the same time. I may never make sense of what happened that day, but I realized that the only way to honor Mike and David's lives was to bring meaning to mine.

I read a card every morning that says, SEIZE THIS MOMENT. It reminds me to concentrate on what's important and to disregard what isn't. It helps me maintain a healthy awareness that this could be my last moment or the last moment for someone I love. There's no time to delay and there's no time to waste.

Life is not a dress rehearsal. I have a finite number of moments and I want to live them as fully as I can. Whenever I feel hurt or angry and am tempted to take it out on someone else, I ask myself: What if this was the last day of my life? Would I want the last thing I said to be insensitive, selfish, or hurtful?

Happiness is not a future date on the calendar. It's now. Now is the time to write that letter, make the phone call or tell people how much I love and appreciate them. And when I live my life that way, the truth of what Mike said so many years ago shines as bright as it did that night, "It doesn't get any better than this."

David Rivers and me
Martha's Vineyard, Massachusetts–July 1972

Patriot Dreams

Reach high, for stars lie hidden in your soul.
Dream deep, for every dream precedes the goal.
—MOTHER TERESA

※

WHENEVER I'M ASKED to reveal one of those fun facts about myself that people probably don't know, I share the time I tried out for the New England Patriots as a walk-on at training camp. I didn't have a prayer of making the roster and I knew it. But when I put on that uniform it felt like every cell in my body was alive with superhuman powers. I was living a dream that transcended reality and I was going to make the most of it.

For two weeks I played every play like it was the last play of my life. If they wanted to, veteran players could handle me physically, but I played with such intensity I suspect they thought I was psychotic. They purposely avoided me and I was able to make some attention-grabbing plays.

On cut-down day, I walked down the hallway to look at the list before I cleaned out my locker, certain I was gone. And that's when I got the greatest surprise of my life. As my eyes scanned the list of the final roster, there it was:

54) Art Dwight

I made the team. I knew it had to be for special teams, but it didn't matter. I was going to play professional football for the New England Patriots, the team I had worshipped since I was seven years old. The ecstasy of this moment was suddenly cut short by a realization that this must be a mistake, an administrative error. But since I was already playing with the house's money, I decided to go for broke and see Coach Bill Belichick.

As I walked onto the practice field, I decided to be up front and humble in hopes that he'd see something in my character that would win him over. He was talking to one of the other coaches when I interrupted him. He looked annoyed. I wasn't off to a good start.

"Coach, I saw my name on the fifty-four-man roster."

He just looked at me.

"I know I don't have the skills..."

"No, you don't," Belichick said, cutting me off. "Perhaps that's why we have a fifty-three-man roster."

And that was it. The end of my dream, literally. I woke up. It was so real and vivid that it took a few minutes to accept that it never actually happened. I can still recall every detail—the sights, sounds and smell of the grass as if it were an actual memory. I can still see my name on that list and the *I can't believe I'm even talking to you* look on Coach Belichick's face when he killed my dream. Twice.

Although the ending was swift and brutal, I wouldn't trade that dream for anything. Like all great dreams it made me feel fully alive. And this one always gets a good laugh when Raquel prompts me to retell it.

I love dreams. They bring power, excitement and meaning to my life. Ever since I was a young boy, despite all of the suffering I experienced and the mistakes I made, I always had a dream of a better life—but not just for me, for everyone. It was this dream, this idea, which always kept me moving forward.

Dreams are the seeds and sparks of every goal or accomplishment. Anything that I've ever achieved that has meaning or significance started first as a dream. No matter how bad things may seem, or how rough it's been, it's always the dream that ignites my imagination and pulls me like a tractor-beam to a better, brighter world.

No, I never played for the New England Patriots, but I did live to see them win their first Super Bowl in New Orleans in February 2002. I also got to hold the Super Bowl trophy with Tedy Bruschi. And Belichick may have saved my life. If I made the team, I would have likely been killed on the first play from scrimmage.

Although my dreams kept me going, it wasn't until later that I learned their true purpose. I may not achieve a dream or a goal the way I imagined it, but that's really not important. It's not the destination that matters; it's how much I learn, change and grow on my way there.

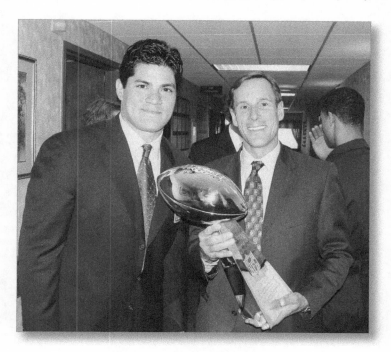

With my "teammate" Tedy Bruschi
Bethesda, Maryland–April 2005

The Right Way

*Success is not dependent on engaging in a certain
business, but by doing things in a certain way.*
—Wallace D. Wattles

I AM A TRAITOR TO my own kind. Perhaps it was the result of growing up with three older sisters, but for whatever reason I've never fit
the typical guy mold. I like shopping, chick flicks, John Denver and
an occasional Barry Manilow tune. There are three things, however,
where I maintain absolute solidarity with my tribe; that grilling,
physical strength and the thing that is performed standing up belong
to the male domain.

Men have defended our exclusive rights to these functions for
centuries. It is an unwritten law that our authority and expertise
are never to be questioned by anyone with XX chromosomes. Any
female involvement might set off a chain of cataclysmic events that
could destroy the natural balance of the sexes and alter the course of
human history. All men share a sacred oath to protect the *secret* of
our supremacy in these areas.

The secret, of course, is that we possess no special skill in these
things whatsoever and that even semi-intelligent animals could be
trained to do it. If this secret were exposed, we would be forced

75

to confront an even greater fear, that we serve no useful purpose. Women could start secretly stockpiling sperm banks—amassing the power to eliminate us at their discretion. Deep down, we also suspect that women find our delusions amusing, but keep us around because someone needs to clean out the cat box or take out the trash. We live in perpetual denial of this possibility.

So it was that I was doing my Perfect Pushups™ one morning with exaggerated grunts and exhalations so my wife could appreciate just how difficult it is, when she said, "You're not going up all the way." *Did she really just say that?* I thought, *did she breach the Man Zone? First there was Eve with the snake, Pandora with the box, Jezebel and the vineyard and now Raquel with the push-ups. Did she really want to join that club?*

But perhaps this was just a little misunderstanding, an innocent oversight. After all, it is permissible to speak to a man while he exercises, with comments such as, "Wow, honey, you are ripped," or "You should be on the cover of *Men's Health*," or "Nice six-pack." But this was like Iraq invading Kuwait; I couldn't just let it go. The only way I could restore the equilibrium that has existed between the sexes for thousands of years was to prove that *she was wrong*—that it was impossible for me to execute an incorrect pushup.

As I frantically searched for the perfect comeback, considering relationship-builder remarks like, *Oh, I'm sorry, when did YOU become a fitness expert?* I could not ignore one stubborn fact—that Raquel is the most observant person I've ever known and disputing her assessments is an exercise in masochism. So with apologies to all men, I did the unthinkable: I surrendered. "You're right," I said, "I'm not going up all the way."

Raquel inspired me to reevaluate everything about my technique. I discovered that my form wasn't straight, there was too much slack and I wasn't going slowly enough to get the full isometric benefit. I did my next set correctly, going up all the way, a difference of maybe an inch, and the effort I needed to expend nearly doubled. I had been doing forty repetitions, but could only complete twenty-five when I did them correctly.

A year later, I've doubled my total to fifty and I am in the best physical shape of my life. I evaluated my pull-up technique and improved that too. I'd been psychologically stuck on a maximum of twelve, the highest I could do in the Marine Corps when I was nineteen-years-old. By doing them the right way, I can now complete sixteen pull-ups, breaking a twenty-eight-year old plateau.

I'm reminded of the razor's edge of difference between success and failure—and that the outcome doesn't depend on doing the right things as much as it does doing the *right things in the right way*. I was doing the right thing by exercising, but I hadn't seen much improvement in nearly twenty years because I wasn't doing it in the right way. The *how* is just as, if not more important, than the *what*.

Whenever I want to improve something in my life, I'm tempted to find the new idea, technique or plan that will solve my problem. I've learned to resist this temptation. I usually don't need a new plan; I just need to execute the one I have correctly. As the saying goes, "If you want a new idea, read an old book."

And for the record, Raquel has never catered to my male ego with comments like, "Wow, honey, you are ripped," but she does continue to offer advice, and I have learned to be open to whatever she says. Maybe she'll even keep me around a little longer. After all, who's going to take out the trash or clean out the cat box?

Confessions of a Sugar Junkie

Losing is gaining.

—Lao Tzu

——— ›‹ ——

I'LL NEVER FORGET THE DAY I realized I was a sugar addict. I had gone three days without sugar and I was decompensating. My cravings fueled desperate thoughts which blurred the line between madness and civilized behavior. *How far would I go for a sugar fix?* I wondered. *Would I lie? Definitely. Cheat? Probably. Steal? Maybe ...*

I had just started the fourth day of the South Beach Diet and the only thing between me and an eight-hundred-calorie chocolate chip cookie was the promise I made to my wife that we would do this together. The diet cruelly corresponded with a family trip to Disney World which was like sending an arsonist to put out a fire.

The land of Mickey for me was no longer a happy little place where dreams come true. As I walked by the endless parade of sweets and ice cream stands, I was beginning to relate to heroin addicts in a way I never thought possible. I thought about dropping to my knees in front of a kiosk, imploring the attendant, "I need to get well, baby. I'll do anything, just give me that cookie."

I wasn't just having a hard time adjusting to this diet, this was withdrawal. I learned that I was more than a sugar junkie; I was a simple carbohydrate junkie. I discovered that processed foods are loaded with sugar. *Loaded.* I started reading the ingredients of the foods I bought and was shocked to learn that sugar is often the second or third highest ingredient in almost everything from salad dressings to tomato sauce, from jelly to peanut butter, breads, juice, yogurt and cereals.

I didn't need a Ph.D to understand that my glycemic levels were sky-high before I threw in my daily dose of cookies and candy, which is like throwing gasoline onto a raging fire. This brought me to a truth about diets and eating habits that changed my life. Diets are temporary. And once I reached my goals, I'd go right back to the habits that got me in trouble to begin with.

My light-bulb moment was realizing that the key to living a healthy, high-energy life was to change my eating habits *permanently*. I transitioned from unhealthy carbs to low-fat proteins, vegetables, salads and fruits—a lifestyle I've kept to this day. These changes have made a dramatic difference in my health, energy and daily feeling of wellness.

But the sugar junkie in me refused to go quietly into the night. All it took were a few exceptions, a dessert here or a piece of chocolate there…and soon I was back in business. Embarrassed by my lack of self-control, I had tried to hide my habit by pretending I was doing something else in the kitchen when I made my sugar raids, sneaking in through the dining room or repositioning trash on top of candy bar wrappers so Raquel wouldn't see it.

And there was nothing like double stuffed Oreos to bring out the full-fledged junkie in me—it was like waving a red flag at a rabid bull—I wanted those Oreos and I didn't care who knew it. A new package would last less than twenty-four hours—a lesson my daughters learned repeatedly when they'd find only crumbs left in the plastic tray.

I doubt there's ever been an intervention for sugar consumption, but when my sister-in-law Pinky told me that she makes sure her house is stocked with cookies and sweets when I visit, I didn't need one. Any delusions about my habit being a secret were gone. I had a problem and it was time to change. I decided it was time to get serious and put a stop to it.

I went cold turkey for six months and am now living mostly sugar free. This gave me the willpower and self-control to have an occasional treat without going off the reservation. That was more than a year ago and it's paid big dividends—my daily energy level is higher and more consistent, I sleep better at night, I feel more alert, focused and more physically relaxed and peaceful than I ever have in my life. I don't owe all of this to eliminating simple sugar, but it was a significant factor.

Now that I'm experiencing the benefits of a mostly sugar-free life, I can see both sides of a fascinating paradox. For more than forty years I couldn't imagine a life without sugar and now I can't imagine a life with it. This begets an obvious question: Why was it so hard to stop?

Years ago, when I read the line "losing is gaining" by the ancient Chinese philosopher Lao Tzu, I thought it made no sense whatsoever. I get it now. When I thought about giving up sugar, I saw it as a sacrifice. The thought of life without carrot cake, chocolate chip cookies, bread pudding or crème brulee was unbearable. I could only think in terms of what I was losing. And when I thought that way, I didn't think I could do it.

But now that I'm on the other side, it's easy to see that what I saw as a loss was really a gain—a huge gain. Once I gave up my emotional attachment to sugar, I was able to make the change and experience the benefits of life without it. It's a much better life for me—and surely an improvement over being on my hands and knees, begging a stranger for a chocolate chip cookie.

Walk a Mile

We hold these truths to be self-evident, that all men are created equal.
—THE DECLARATION OF INDEPENDENCE

———— ⚶ ————

WHEN I WAS A SENIOR MANAGER at *The Gazette* newspaper, I read an article on diversity which reported that there were only ten women CEOs of Fortune 500 Companies, which meant that *two percent* of the top companies in the United States were run by women. I was shocked. Since women comprised at least half of the workforce, I naively assumed that there was a corresponding degree of progress in the higher ranks.

I thought the "people" responsible for this should be charged, tried and sent to prison. I was thinking about this during a meeting with my white male boss and our two white male group presidents when it hit me—I'm one of "them." I made myself a promise to do what I could to change this imbalance. My best contribution was developing and mentoring a female manager who later took my position and is doing a far better job than I ever did.

My diversity education took a quantum leap three years later when I attended a leadership program for Navy spouses, which went concurrently with my wife's pre-command course. When I stepped into the room for the first time, it was hard not to notice that I was the only man out of thirty women. For the first time in my life, I got a small taste of what it felt like to be in the minority.

Throughout the week it was, "Ladies this" and "Ladies that." When we left the room it was always, "Ladies, don't forget your purses." Being called a lady was an enlightening experience, but it can't compare to what my friend Greg Wagner experienced when his wife Elaine was the commanding officer of the Naval Hospital in Beaufort, South Carolina. At a formal banquet, he was seated at the head table next to a Marine Corps general with a name card that read, Mrs. Wagner.

Being "one of the girls" was an eye-opening experience, but then I considered what my wife was going through in the room next door. Not only was she the only woman in a room of thirty men, but she was one of two minorities. And while my experience was a first for me, this is something Raquel has dealt with her entire life.

Raquel talked about how difficult it had been for her as a woman and a minority in a white-male dominated profession. At the time I thought I understood, but I didn't have a clue until I stepped into that room of women and realized that one of these things was not like the other—and it was me. I was the odd ball. I experienced a seismic shift in awareness. I finally got it.

I got it because I *experienced* it. I could spend the rest of my life learning about discrimination, but not until I lived it could I truly comprehend it. There are some things in life that can only be grasped through experience, like the death of a loved one or the birth of a child.

When I criticized people as a boy, my father was quick to remind me never to judge someone until I walked a mile in his or her shoes. If I truly want to understand what someone else is going through, then I must be willing to find a way to see, experience or understand things as they do. Opinions without experience, knowledge or aware-ness are anemic things. In other words, Art, if you don't know what they're going through, keep your mouth shut.

As I reflected on Raquel's experience, I realized that I had an extremely narrow view of diversity. I had a box-checking viewpoint of it such as male or female, race, age or sexual orientation. It occurred to me that true diversity encompasses *everything* that is unique to each one of us—our backgrounds, heritage, beliefs, culture, skills, gifts, intelligence, feelings, etc. It's virtually unlimited.

Looking at these qualities as differences creates separation between me and the other person. This perception, even if it's not negative, makes me part of the problem. The solution is for me to do everything I can to live by the "self-evident" truth that all of us are created equal. I need to do more than just accept other people for their unique qualities—I need to embrace them.

I have a long way to go on this journey, but critically examining my challenge is a step in the right direction. Keeping my week as "a lady" fresh in my mind serves as a reminder of how difficult it is for others and the obstacles they've had to overcome just to be considered *equal.*

My first experiment with diversity
Wayland, Massachusetts–1973

It's Questionable

I've looked at life from both sides now, from win and lose, and still somehow, it's life's illusions I recall, I really don't know life, at all.
—Joni Mitchell

◆

SHORTLY AFTER I WROTE MY first book, I was preparing a talk for the local rotary club on truth when I discovered something that discredited everything I planned to say. I was thinking about tie-ins for the theme of my talk "Is it the Truth?" when I happened to glance at the back cover of my book. In my short biography it said I was the president of *Dwight & Associates, Inc.*, a "highly sought-after speaker" and that my audio programs were "among the best available today."

Those assertions may have sounded impressive, but they weren't even in the same zip code as the truth. I didn't have any "associates," I wasn't being "sought after" by anyone and I'm not sure how my audio programs could be the "best available today" when they didn't even exist. I was building my business on personal authenticity and there I was a big, fat liar on the back cover of my own book.

By the time my wife came home that night, I was in a DEFCON ONE emotional meltdown. All was lost. I could never sell my book, appear in public or make an income in this business. I was a failure, a disgrace, and a charlatan. When I asked Raquel what she thought I should do she said, "Read your book."

What?! I thought. *Did you not hear what I just explained to you? Exactly what about my life being over did you not understand? Do you need me to rewind the tape?* But what she said was so unexpected it interrupted my temper tantrum just enough for me to stop and question what was really going on, which was that my perception was negative and out of proportion to the situation.

The next day, I took her advice. I read my book and found what I needed to hear. My problem wasn't my material; it was the back cover copy of my book. What I wrote on the back cover was the result of my marketing background, where I developed a habit of embellishment to compel people to buy. The book was authentic—I just needed to change my promotional strategy to reflect that.

In less than twenty-four hours my life went from all is lost to all is well. What changed? The only thing that changed was my *perception* of my situation. Perception, to me, is one of the most intriguing human qualities because *everything* (except truth) is perception. Every thought I think, emotion I feel or opinion I have is my perception—it is not a fact and it is not the truth—it is simply my *point of view.*

And the exciting thing about this discovery for me is that any point of view is *subjective* and therefore *subject* to change. My world is a composite of what I think, feel and believe, so if I don't like what's happening in my world—all I need to do is change my point of view. So whenever something "goes wrong" in my life, I know I can change it. I start with the most powerful tool in my how-to-change tool kit, a question.

A question interrupts my current pattern of thinking. If I'm having negative thoughts about a person or a situation, a question forces me to pause and reevaluate what I'm thinking and why I'm thinking it. An effective question engages my intellect while simultaneously cooling down my emotions. My mind is an extraordinary instrument, but only when I put it to work.

When I ask myself a question, it puts my mind on a search to *find the answer for myself.* Questioning is the key to learning because once I ask and answer my own question, I'm ready to accept a new truth. If I get advice, read or hear something, it may help me, but it doesn't have the power to change me like a question.

There are many powerful questions, but here are a few of my favorites:

- What is the truth?
- What can I learn from this?
- Have I accepted one hundred percent ownership for my thoughts, feelings and actions?
- How can I be helpful in this situation?
- How will this situation improve my life and the lives of others?
- Am I seeing this situation or person through the eyes of love?
- What's the worst that could happen?
- Is this something I should try to change or accept?

When I use these questions, they have never failed to re-frame my perspective or find a better answer that benefits my life and everyone involved. Conversely, whenever I've failed to interrupt my thinking or allowed negative emotions to carry the day—the outcome has *never once* been positive or constructive. I will never solve a problem with a negative answer.

It's a sobering fact that everything on earth is either in a state of growth or decline. We're either growing or dying, creating or disintegrating. Regardless of my physical age, I'll never stop growing intellectually, emotionally or spiritually—as long as I continue to question everything.

The Golden Law

Life is a perpetual instruction in cause and effect.
—RALPH WALDO EMERSON

⊷ ⊰⊱ ⊶

I LOST MY JOB BECAUSE Aly woke up late one day.

I had to drive her to school which made me late for work. When I got to work, I was fired. As a result, we couldn't afford to eat, but all wasn't lost because our neighbors invited us to dinner. I don't remember any of this, but that's exactly how Aly says it happened in her fictional fourth grade assignment on the law of cause and effect.

Aly's teacher, Mrs. Brown, gave her an "Excellent! √+" for this assignment. I'm not sure I want to know her psychological motivation for picking me to lose my job, but nonetheless, at nine years old, she succinctly captured a lesson that's taken me a lifetime to master. That there is a direct correlation between everything I think, say and do (the cause) and what happens in my life and the lives of others (the effect).

In Aly's example, just one mistake led to a sequence of consequences for herself and everyone in her family. Granted, it was a bit extreme, but the application of the law is dead-bang accurate. The results aren't always as apparent as they are in this case, but everything I think, say or do will affect me and other people just as surely as the night precedes the day.

Cause and effect is a *law* because it is scientifically verifiable; for every cause there is an effect, and for every effect, a cause. Ralph Waldo Emerson called it the "law of laws" because everything in our world, and the universe, is subject to its principles. Nothing is exempt, including me.

It's a perfect formula to live my life by, which is why I call it the "Golden Law." According to this law every good thought, feeling, or action produces good results and every bad thought, feeling, or action produces bad results. If I follow this law—it is virtually impossible for things to "go wrong" in my life.

My understanding and application of this law was one of the most important things that turned my life around. I realized that it was my choices that determined my life—and it didn't matter what happened in my past—I could change my life by making decisions in accordance with this law.

Once I got this I could no longer blame my circumstances on a rough childhood, a bad relationship, or anything else. The law of cause and effect applies to everyone equally. If I jump off a building, for example, the law of gravity is going to take me down. I could complain that no one told me about the law, or that I didn't understand it, but I'm still going down.

The law tells me that the results in my life are directly proportionate to my effort. If I put a little bit in, I'm going to get a little bit out. But if I put a lot into life—I'm going to get a lot out of it. It's my choice, and it's entirely within my control.

To have the life that I want means all I have to do is abide by this Golden Law. So losing my hypothetical job wasn't such a bad thing after all. Thanks Aly, and special thanks to her teacher, Mrs. Brown, for helping her students learn and apply this law at such an early age.

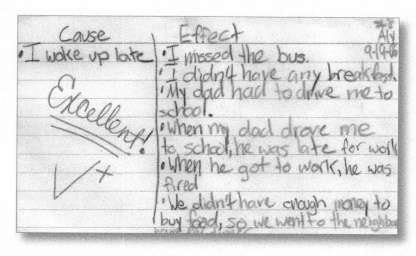

Aly's original note
Germantown, Maryland–September 2006

It's Never too Late

It's never too late to become the person you might have been.
—George Eliot

⊷—⊶◆⊰—⊷

ONE SENTENCE changed my life.

I was half-asleep during a seminar when the speaker said, "The quality of our lives depends on the quality of our relationships." This was an absolute statement that ignited my curiosity as well as my skepticism. *Could this be true? Is the quality of my life really determined by the quality of my relationships?* I was so intrigued by this statement that I invested years of study and practice to prove or disprove it.

In any relationship, past or present, I realized that every positive thought, feeling or action toward that person did indeed improve the quality of my life. On the other side of the coin, every negative thought, feeling or action toward another person detracted from the quality of my life. I don't think I'll win a Pulitzer for this insight, but the implications for me were compelling.

As I considered all of the relationships in my life, I could see how the people I didn't feel good about were bringing me down and that the people I did feel good about were lifting me up. Following this simple logic, I asked myself: What kind of life could I have if I didn't have any negativity or conflict in my relationships? I would have something that had been eluding me for most of my life: psychological and emotional freedom.

As I started my journey toward this goal, I drew two pie charts in my journal. One represented my mind as it was then (my starting point) and the other what I wanted my mind to be (my goal). In my first chart, I estimated that sixty percent of my thoughts and feelings were negative and forty percent were positive. My target chart included a ten percent slice for negative thoughts and a ninety percent slice for positive thoughts and feelings. *How amazing my life would be if I could achieve that goal.*

I wrote a list of every relationship in my life that was eliciting unhealthy thoughts or emotions. Knowing that the only thing I needed to concern myself with was my thoughts, feelings or actions, I asked myself what I was doing, or what I did, to contribute to the problem. I knew that any temptation to project my issues or put the blame onto the other person would lead to failure. I had to take one hundred percent ownership.

Starting with my family, friends and business associates, every time I had a negative thought or judgment, I told myself, "This isn't about them. It's about me. What do I need to change?" As my perceptions of others changed, I continued to feel better. I was improving my life one relationship at a time. My negative slice of the pie was shrinking and my positive slice was growing.

Finding peace with past relationships, however, proved a greater challenge because I didn't have any interaction with them. Whenever I thought about people I hurt in the past I experienced guilt or remorse, but I didn't know where to start or what I could do about it. I couldn't turn back the hands of time, but my heart wanted healing and closure.

I had a close friend sophomore year in high school, but when some of my classmates started harassing him because he was a serious student, I didn't defend him. Worse, I joined them in taunting him. I betrayed him and he never spoke to me again. A friend of mine ran into him at college years later and asked him if he knew Art Dwight when he learned he went to Deerfield Academy. "Don't ever say that name again," was his response.

It was a devastating confirmation of how much I had hurt my friend. I had found peace with my past in many other ways, but this was an albatross, an enduring reminder of the pain I had caused other people through my actions. I didn't deserve or have any expectation that I could make this relationship right, but I needed to at least try.

I wrote him a heart felt letter apologizing for my actions and expressing my regret. I didn't expect or receive a response. In my role as captain of our class, I included personal notes to him with any class correspondence over the ensuing years. Every time I reached out to him, I felt better. I knew I was doing the only thing I could.

About five years later, I was working at my desk when an email from him popped onto my screen. It felt like Heaven had hacked into my network. His note was casual, warm and friendly—as if we had kept in touch on a regular basis. There was no mention of the past or my apology, and it wasn't necessary. His email erased any remaining guilt or self-recrimination that I felt. It was finally time to move on.

I had a similar experience with a friend freshman year of high school. I played a joke on him that I thought was pretty funny according to my immature, adolescent way of thinking, but by any objective measure it was reprehensible and disgusting. He didn't find the humor in it. He punched me a few times before our classmates broke it up.

The next day I saw him with a cast on his arm. He broke his hand during our fight. I felt really bad. When I tried to apologize, he turned away from me. We went through three more years of high school together without saying another word to each other. His hand would heal, but the break in our friendship would not.

Twenty-seven years later I saw him for the first time since high school at a memorial service for one of our classmates. He was standing right behind me. This was my chance. I turned to him and told him how sorry I was for I what did and for what happened to our friendship. "No, it was my fault," he said. We spontaneously hugged each other, bringing healing and closure to an ancient rift.

Reconciling with my friends after all those years lifted a weight off my heart and conscience. I realized that *every* unhealthy relationship was weighing me down as if I were carrying a brick. Every time I improved a relationship or reconciled a damaged one, I could let that brick go. One by one, a weight was lifted, freeing up precious mental and emotional space for the things that truly matter: love, joy, and peace.

It's never too late to make a change in any relationship no matter how bad it's been or hopeless it seems. I just need to find the peace in my own heart first, let go of any negativity toward the other person, and resolve to do whatever I can to make it right. The path to peace is always open if I have the courage to look at and face my own "stuff."

I have to always keep working at it, but looking at my pie chart today, my positive slice of the pie is even greater than ninety percent—proof that I'm happier and healthier than I've ever been—and that the quality of my life does indeed depend on the quality of my relationships.

Believe It or Not

ON OUR WAY TO SCHOOL one morning Aly was talking about one of her favorite Disney movies. "You know, Dad, Pocahontas didn't marry John Smith, she actually ended up with an Indian chief."

"I hate to tell you this, Aly," I replied, "But she didn't marry either one of them. She married an Englishman, John Rolfe, accompanied him to England, got sick, and died a year later."

"Oh that's just great!" Aly indignantly blurted out. "My *entire* childhood has been a lie. Santa Claus, the Easter Bunny, all lies! What's next? Was George Washington even President?"

I wanted to burst out laughing, but to Aly this was a serious matter. Her feelings of betrayal were real. It can be a shocking and painful process to try and reconcile stories we love and believe with the truth, a rite of passage that can foster doubt, mistrust and cynicism.

I could relate to Aly's experience. I won't forget the day I learned that Christopher Plummer was lip synching "Edelweiss." This deception motivated me to question everything else about the so-called "true story" of the *Sound of Music*. By the time I finished my investigation my naïve belief in fairy tales was on life support.

There were actually ten Von Trapp children, not seven; the names, sexes and ages of the children were changed, Maria and Captain Von Trapp were married in 1927, not 1938, and they never hiked over the mountains to Switzerland, fleeing instead on a train with papers, to Italy. Worst of all, Maria had a ferocious temper and said in an interview that she didn't even love Captain Von Trapp at the time, but did it for the children.

As Aly and I are learning, there are often discrepancies between our beliefs and the truth and the process of reconciling the two is ongoing. As upsetting as it can be, however, I've found that letting go of my old beliefs is essential to my personal growth, peace of mind, and happiness.

When faced with information that conflicts with what I believe to be true, I've learned the hard way that stubbornly clinging to my old beliefs and/or denying, attacking or discrediting other points of view is an unhealthy exercise. This isn't an opinion. It's a fact. I know. I've done it.

If I'm not willing to at least examine other ideas or points of view, I won't learn, grow or change. I'm a prisoner locked in a cell, serving a self-imposed sentence of ignorance and stagnation. But the exciting thing about this cell is that I have the key to open it—and to escape to a life of freedom without fear of capture. This key is an open mind.

When I hear something I disagree with, instead of responding with thoughtful comments such as, "That's a lie!" "You're wrong *and* you're an idiot," I ask myself, *am I certain that my idea is the truth?* This does two things. 1) It puts my response on hold. 2) It interrupts my conditioned way of thinking and forces me to *think* and critically examine my ideas.

This process rips the lid off my mind, stimulates my imagination and opens up a world of growth, change, and endless possibilities. Instead of feeling upset or betrayed because what I once believed wasn't accurate, I feel liberated and excited to embrace a new and creative way of thinking.

I saw that my old ideas were blocking new ideas, ideas that had the potential to change my life. That's why I strive to always keep my mind open to new ideas and new ways of looking at things. In any given moment of any day lies the potential for a new insight or discovery that can change my life—if I'm willing to look.

When Right is Wrong

*Nothing is more conducive to peace of mind
than not having any opinions at all.*
—GEORG CHRISTOPH LICHTENBERG

⊶ ⚔ ⊷

D URING ALY'S FIFTH-GRADE promotion ceremony, comments from other classmates were read aloud as they crossed the stage. One of Aly's classmates wrote, "Aly is as bright as a falling star." During the drive home, Aly proudly re-read her comments, but when she got to the one about the falling star, Grace couldn't restrain herself, declaring, "I learned this in science class, falling stars aren't that bright. In fact, they're actually dying."

"Falling stars are bright!" Aly insisted.

"No, they're not. They're falling because they *are* dying."

"That's not true!"

"No, Aly, it is. In fact, the stars are already dead, *like you*, which is what your classmates were trying to tell you."

The harder Aly tried to defend, the more determined Grace was to prove her wrong. As the battle escalated, decorum deteriorated. Once they exhausted everything they could think of about falling stars, their verbal grenades got increasingly personal and irrelevant to the original topic.

There was a familiar desperation to this battle, as neither Grace nor Aly showed any restraint or willingness to compromise. What they didn't know is that they were fighting a battle that neither one of them could ever win. It was an all-too-familiar reminder for me of my own communication struggles.

Growing up and even into my adult life, being *right* was a matter of great importance. I invested a lot of time and energy preparing my arguments, gathering facts, positions and coming up with the *killer point*—the verbal kryptonite that would obliterate my opponent's argument, bringing them to their knees, awed by my acumen, sagacity, and superior logic. I didn't just prepare this stuff, I obsessed over it. I spent hours writing down my points and practicing my delivery.

Alas, despite all this preparation my confrontations never went as planned. No one seemed impressed with my points, nor did anyone ever say, "That's a brilliant argument, Art, you are right and I was so wrong. How could I be so stupid? Will you forgive me?"

In reality, the other person would invariably blindside me with something I hadn't prepared for. *Oh (expletive)!* I'd think. *This discredits my entire argument.* When that happened, I was so obsessed with prevailing, I sometimes continued to argue my points even though I *knew* I was wrong. How pathetic is that?

But I didn't always lose. Sometimes when all was seemingly lost, I'd return fire with a comeback so pithy and powerful it would drop my opponent like an undefended right hook. *Boo-yah! In your face, sucker!* I'd raise my arms up in victory! I was the winner! I was right! It was a perfect moment. I just wish I wasn't alone when it happened in the shower or on the treadmill. If you can wait at least three days for the perfect comeback, I'm your man.

Time and experience mellowed my compulsion for winning arguments, possibly because I never did. But it wasn't until I learned something from Axialent's Fred Kofman that I got it like I was holding up a metal bar during a lightning storm. Kofman said that when we insist on being right it means that someone else must be wrong. The scales dropped from my eyes.

No wonder I used to have so much conflict in my life! Even if I had the best intentions, I was constantly putting people on the defensive. I got pushback because they were feeling like I was trying to prove them wrong. I flashed back to so many failed discussions at home or work and realized that my *opinions* were the source of the problem. I was so focused on my need to justify my point of view that I failed to consider what the other person might be thinking or feeling.

In a contest of opinions, nobody wins because it will never build consensus or trust. I thought of all the times I was in business meetings when it was obvious that no one felt good about the decision, but whoever had the power (sometimes me) would slam something through. I realized that in a room of ten people, there will be ten different opinions—and although there may be some alignment—there will always be differences.

There is no right or wrong when it comes to opinions because all opinions are subjective. Opinions are not facts. They are subject to change and often do, so anytime I presented an opinion as fact only revealed my ignorance of this basic truth.

I still need to tell myself to drop my need to be right and truly listen to what the other person is thinking and feeling. This is a key to effective communication. It reminds me of something that Marianne Williamson wrote once, "Do you want to be right or do you want to be happy?" I want to be happy. And dropping my need to be right is a good first step in that direction.

Grace & Aly
Lyme, New Hampshire–July 2009

That's so Rude!

*There cannot be greater rudeness than to interrupt
another in the current of his discourse.*
—JOHN LOCKE

THE MARK OF A TRUE FRIEND is someone who will slap you across
the face when you need it. Trina Lapier is that kind of friend.
We were having lunch together when my phone buzzed with a text
message. I reflexively checked the message and started texting back.
"That's so rude!" Trina said with unvarnished honesty.

I bristled.

My feelings were hurt and I wanted to strike back in some way—to
prove that what she said wasn't true. But I learned a long time ago
that defensiveness means there must be something going on with me
that I'm not willing to see or admit. This kept my ego in check long
enough to think about what she said and realize that I had no defense.

"You're right," I conceded. "It is rude and I'm sorry." What Trina
didn't know is that Grace hadn't been feeling well and I was on standby
to pick her up from school. However, that doesn't excuse or change
the fact that we were in the middle of a conversation when I grabbed
my cell phone to start a conversation with someone else.

Ordinarily, I leave my phone in the car whenever I attend a meeting to avoid what happened, but the larger take-away is the importance of giving whoever I'm with my full attention. If someone is talking to me and I'm thinking about something else, looking around the room, interrupting them, texting or picking up a phone call, I am giving that person less than my full attention. Or in Trina's vernacular, I'm being rude.

Rudeness to me is the opposite of two values I treasure, honor and respect. If I'm committed to honoring and respecting other people then my behavior should reflect that.

Whenever I talk to someone in person or on the phone, I make a conscious effort to remind myself that this person is important and that they deserve my full attention. When I focus on something it's hard for me to switch gears, so if someone calls or needs my attention, I say to myself, "Be present, Art, and listen."

The last thing I need is a cell phone, iPod or other technologies to distract me more than I already am which means I need to work even harder to keep them from interfering with my relationships. There's little difference between responding to a text message while I'm talking to someone else and abruptly walking away in the middle of a conversation. Not only am I failing to honor and respect that person, but I'm sending him an unspoken message that I am more interested in someone else's text than what he has to say.

As charity begins at home, so does my decision to honor and respect others. After my lunch with Trina and some time for reflection, I realized that I was even guiltier of not being completely present with my wife and children. Just in case I didn't get the memo during my lunch with Trina, Aly said to me a week later, "Dad, you're not listening. You say that you are, but I can always tell when you're not."

That's why my decision to honor and respect has to apply to everyone. If I change my texting behavior depending on who I am with, what does that say about me? It means that I'm deciding to honor and respect some people, but not others. And that's worse than rude.

But when I am completely present and focused with another person I am able to listen, validate, and appreciate him or her. When my focus isn't divided, I see and learn things about the other person that I would've missed before. I am giving them honor and respect. I am telling them, "I value you. I care. You are important to me."

Label Damage

Labels are for filing. Labels are for clothing.
Labels are not for people.
—MARTINA NAVRATILOVA

❖ ❖

GETTING INFORMATION FROM my teenage daughter is like getting a presidential candidate to talk candidly about entitlement
programs. On the way to a concert with Grace and her friend Brett, I
was trying to understand why I was dropping them off at 3 p.m. when
the concert started at 7 p.m. I don't usually try to make sense of these
things, but I was concerned for their safety. The actual conversation
took about twenty minutes, but here is an excerpt:

"But honey, I don't understand, the gates won't open until 6 p.m."

"That's right, but I need to get there early."

"I get that, but you have assigned seats, right?"

"Yes, but we still need to be there at 3 p.m."

"But why do you need to be there at 3 p.m?"

"We just do."

"But there won't be anyone there. What's the point?"

(Heavy sigh) "Because I want to see John when he arrives,
okaaaaay?"

"John? Who's John?"

"The lead singer of The Maine, don't you know anything?!"

"Oh, I get it, you're a groupie."

"I AM NOT A GROUPIE!" shouted Grace.

In a valiant effort to defuse a conversation headed in the wrong direction, Brett chimed in, "I'm a groupie. In fact, I have a t-shirt that says 'Groupie in search of a band.'"

(Softly and grudgingly) Grace admitted, "Okay, I guess maybe I am a groupie."

The light finally dawned on my marble head. Grace was reluctant to share her true intentions with me because she was trying to avoid precisely what happened, being labeled as a groupie. Of all people, I should be careful not to label others because I know first-hand how damaging it can be.

On my first day of junior high school a group of bullies called me a geek. I had never heard that word before, but I knew it wasn't a compliment and it didn't feel good. And that was just the beginning—for the next two years I was a called a queer, wimp, dork, fag, loser and worse. Those words hurt every time they said it—and it felt like each one took away a piece of my self-confidence.

There wasn't much left of my self-esteem by the time I arrived at Deerfield Academy for high school, but I was determined to make sure no one knew it. After two years on the receiving end of abuse, I started dishing it out. I think my unconscious reasoning was that if I was an aggressor, I could avoid becoming a victim. I picked on other kids for taking their studies seriously or if they were different in some way. I hated myself for it, but I didn't stop either.

Years later, I did an exercise where I counted the labels (a.k.a. judgments) I was making about other people for a day. I included any opinion about another person good, bad or neutral, what they do, what they look like etc. I found that I was making so many judgments I had a hard time finding a thought that wasn't a judgment. It was shocking to see how judgments were dominating my thought patterns, but it was also exciting because it was something I knew I could change.

I saw in a new light how my judgments were affecting my relationships. It is impossible to see someone for who they truly are if a judgment is in the way. My judgments were defining and limiting people—reducing all that is great about another human being, their thoughts, feelings, gifts and spirit, to a one-word summary.

My judgments were a barrier to healthy relationships, yet that is what I wanted. So I took the next step, to explore the genesis of those judgments—a face-slapping process that forced me to realize that my judgments of others were actually judgments of myself. This was a difficult and painful insight to accept, but once I did, I knew I was on the verge of a major shift that could dramatically improve my relationships and my life.

I made a commitment to reduce or eliminate my judgments of others. Whenever a judgment arose, I turned it around to myself, "This isn't about her/him, it's about me." This was hard. But it got easier with practice. My judgments started gradually fading and with them any lingering resentment or anger I had for others or myself. Once I removed the labels, I could see people in a completely new way. I could appreciate, understand, love, and accept them.

I had made progress, but a year later I was ranting about a certain political commentator when Raquel reminded me about my commitment to not judge others. *Ouch*. My judgment of him was no better than his judgment of others. I was basically judging his judgments, which was giving birth to more judgments. It didn't matter what my opinion was—I needed to respect and honor his right to say whatever he wanted to.

There was a time when my relationships with just about everyone, my parents, siblings, friends or coworkers were strained, in conflict or unhealthy in some way. Today I can't think of one relationship where I feel that way. My relationships aren't problem free, of course, but seeing people without judgment helps me resolve conflict faster and without negativity.

In the end, releasing judgment is really about learning how to accept people for *who they are*—not as I want them to be. Accepting others isn't saying, "You know, I accept you." That's a sure sign that I don't. It's an internal shift that comes from my heart. I do my best to allow every person to be who they are and make their own choices. This creates the space for trust to grow and for the relationship to thrive.

It's a wonderful gift to give someone, but in the process I got a gift, too—I can accept others because I finally learned how to accept myself.

Grace and Brett at the concert
St. Augustine, Florida–March 2008

A Change of Heart

————— ✠ —————

I N ANY RELATIONSHIP the moment I think the problem is the other person and not me, it's a flashing neon sign that it's most definitely me. Just before moving to Florida for three years in 2005, a year-long custody battle with Grace and Aly's mom essentially resolved nothing (the court ordered that joint custody remain as it was) and disagreements over scheduling, child support, summer camps, and health care deteriorated to the point where we stopped communicating with each other altogether.

This was a painful chapter of my life. It went against everything I believed about how divorced parents should behave in order to keep children emotionally healthy and secure. Moreover, although I was content with most of the other areas of my life, my inability to "solve" this relationship had me questioning my credibility in my work. One of my core beliefs is that I can't help someone with something I can't do myself—and this relationship gave me a nagging feeling that I was inauthentic.

To that end, I felt that I did everything possible to repair our relationship. I emptied the playbook. I wrote heartfelt letters, made concessions and repeatedly tried for a fresh start, but nothing eased the underlying tension. It only continued to get worse. I became frustrated, angry and increasingly convinced that it must be *her* problem—that she was the one who needed to change.

Grace, fourteen, apparently did not share my assessment of the situation. When I made a comment about something being her mother's responsibility, she blurted out, "I wish the two of you would just grow up, act like adults, and get along." *The two of you?* I thought, *surely she misspoke. Did she just tell the Self-Help Guru to grow up? A man who should be canonized, not criticized, for his superhuman relationship-building efforts?*

But there were two things about that moment that I could not ignore. One, my teenage daughter had just put enough words together to make a complete sentence. Two, it wasn't just her courageous and honest words, but the pain in her voice that flooded me with guilt. As much as I wanted to pin the whole thing on her mother, I knew she was right. She was seeing something that I hadn't been ready or willing to admit.

Grace's comment also forced me to face something I had been avoiding since I returned from Florida a year earlier. In the three years I was away, our relationship had changed. While we had seen each other once a month during that period, it wasn't enough to bridge the uncomfortable distance between us. I didn't ask her about it because I think I was afraid of the answer. When I finally did, what she said crushed me, "Dad, I really hated you."

I had done the one thing I wanted *not* to do as a parent; hurt my children. I couldn't turn back the hands of time, but I could do something about the ongoing conflict with her mother. I didn't want to acknowledge it before, but I knew that in any conflict each person owns a part of it or else the conflict wouldn't exist. I had to put everything on the table and find out what my piece was so I could make things right.

But as I thought about what I could do about it, I was out of answers. I honestly believed that I had tried everything. For one of the few times in my life, I felt hopeless. As I cried, I thought of a prayer I used to say to myself, "Let there be a change and let it begin with me." And that's when the lights came back on.

I realized that I wasn't accepting my ex-wife for who she was or the decisions she was making as Grace and Aly's mother. I was critical, judgmental and angry. Our perpetual conflict was a direct result of my own fear. I wanted certain things for Grace and Aly, but in the process I was judging their mother and contributing to the problem.

The change, as it always does, begins with me. I needed a complete and radical change of heart. I decided to let go of every issue of contention between us and to start honoring and accepting her unconditionally. I made the decision not to fight or contest her parenting decisions. It takes only one person to end a war—and it was time for this war to end.

The moment I made this decision, I could feel years of pent up anger and frustration wash away like water behind a dam under pressure that finally gives way. I knew that everything would be okay. It usually takes years for this kind of transformation, but the truth is I had been working at it for years. I just had the wrong approach.

My change in heart was put to the test less than two weeks later when she sued me for full legal and physical custody. During our court-ordered mediation, I remained calm and comfortable in her presence. I felt no animosity, anger or fear. She gave me five demands and I agreed to all of them. When the mediator asked me for my list of issues, I told her I didn't have any. I didn't even ask her to drop her lawsuit.

Both my ex-wife and the mediator appeared visibly dumbstruck. My ex-wife was expecting a fight and didn't get one and the mediator had nothing to mediate. As for me I felt like everything was right in the world. Somehow I knew that it was over—all those years of conflict, pain, and uncertainty were gone and would never return.

The next day, she called and asked to meet with me without a mediator. We met in Starbucks and quickly reached agreement on everything that had been an issue between us for the last seven years. She even agreed to support the things that were important to me. She dropped the lawsuit and we haven't had one problem of consequence since.

It was my time to pick up the girls so I went to her house and we continued our discussion at her kitchen table. When Grace came home from school and saw us together she was too flummoxed to speak coherently, "What ... huh ... how," she stammered. And then finally, "Will someone please tell me what it is going on?!"

Grace had the courage to open her heart and tell her father to grow up. This gave me the courage to confront the truth and to repay her gift to me with a gift of my own: peace with her mother.

Thank you, Grace. Maybe, just maybe, your dad is growing up.

With Grace at Green Mountain Coffee
Waterbury, Vermont–July 2009

A Puppet on a String

I am, indeed, a king, because I know how to rule myself.
—Pietro Aretino

⊷—≡✦≡—⊶

I GOT SOME UNEXPECTED NEWS from a family member a few months ago and I did something I hadn't done in years. I sent an email criticizing her for what she did. Worse, I received a phone call from another family member and I dragged her into too. And before you can say "family drama," I was at the epicenter of a family firestorm of my own making.

This was a sobering moment for me. I thought I had moved beyond this, but here I was doing something I often advise my clients not to do. So I put myself in a "time out" and thought about what happened. I realized that my feelings were hurt, and I reacted emotionally rather than take a moment to think things through. It was a textbook reminder to *always* stop and think before responding.

Indeed, as I reflected on the mistakes I've made in my life (which conservatively must total in the hundreds of thousands), it occurred to me that every single one could have been avoided if I had taken a moment to stop and think first. I could not think of one insensitive comment, angry reaction, or impulsive decision where I looked back and thought, *Good one, Art. That really improved things.*

It occurred to me that after about thirty years of conflict, drama and avoidable stress that I might want to stop doing that. The answer was ridiculously simple—all I needed was to develop enough self-control to give myself the time to make a better decision before I respond. And oftentimes, the best answer I've found is to not respond at all.

Another insight that helped me overcome my propensity to shoot first and ask questions later, was the realization that when I react emotionally to what another person says or does I become a puppet on a string. If I react without thinking I'm allowing another person to determine my response. I am giving him or her control of my actions, and I am not in control of my own life. *Why would I ever want to do that?*

This fueled my love affair with the power of choice. I *always* have a choice. But I knew that before I could use this great power to my benefit I would first have to understand and control my emotional reactions. This was no small task, but I've learned that the key was to accept that my emotional response belongs to me alone—and that no one else causes it or is responsible for it.

Emotional self-understanding and control gave me insight into the actions of others. When I'm angry, for example, what's really going on is that my feelings are hurt. So when someone is angry, I look past the anger to see the pain. The intensity of the anger reflects the depth of the wound. Seeing someone as hurt, instead of angry, changes my perspective and summons up compassion, empathy, and love for that person.

I've also learned to separate the behavior from the person. What someone says or does is not who they *are*. I've done and said many things over the years that I wish I hadn't, but it wasn't because I was a bad person—I was a wounded person. I don't think anyone ever dreamed as a child, "When I grow up, I want to be so passive aggressive that nobody wants to be around me!"

No one *wants* to be like that, they just don't have the awareness or self-understanding to change their behavior. And the last thing they need is for me to add more negativity or judgment into their life.

In any family, place of business, or organization it seems that someone always has their hair on fire about something. In my experience, emotional negativity and drama causes far more pain and suffering than the situation itself. I have personally seen families and organizations torn apart by it.

I wish I could stop this from happening, but I've learned that getting involved is like wrestling a pig in the mud, pretty soon no one can tell the difference between me and the pig. To avoid this from happening, I try to see myself as a witness and not a participant. It helps me keep my objectivity as well as my peace of mind.

Wayne Dyer said once in a talk that he sees the people he finds challenging as his spiritual masters—whatever they bring up for him is his issue to solve—it has nothing to do with the people that make him crazy. He's right. In the end, it all comes down to a choice: Do I want to have control of my life or do I want others to control it for me? Every time I remember to ask this question, I make the right choice and avoid becoming a puppet on a string.

No Strings Attached

Agape love: (n.) *Unselfish, loyal and benevolent concern for another.*
—WEBSTER'S

THE FIRST TIME I HEARD the word *agape* (pronounced uh-gop-ay), I thought it was a Greek snack dip. For those familiar with the term, that definition may seem a bit limited since agape is an ancient expression of the highest, purest form of sacrificial love. I felt a bit foolish, but at least I was half-right—it is a *Greek* word. And what if it was a *really good* snack dip?

The next time I heard about *agape* was during a lunch with Dave Dabney, a good friend and the common-law mayor of Bethesda, Maryland. "You have to see the movie *Fireproof* with your wife," he said. "It's changed my life and my marriage." The acting, he cautioned, wasn't Academy Award caliber, but he said it was one of the most powerful movies he'd ever seen.

What stayed with me wasn't what Dave said, it was how he said it. It was his passion and conviction that touched my heart and convinced me that we had to see the movie. With three teenage daughters, however, it would be easier to book a lunch with Elvis than find a time for the two of us to see a movie together, but we finally saw it six months later on DVD.

The film revolves around a young couple's struggle to save a marriage teetering on the edge of divorce. The main character's father gives him a forty-day manifesto, a Love Dare, and urges him to not to agree to a divorce until he finishes it. Each day covers an aspect of love followed by a dare to follow through on the lesson it conveyed. Inspired by the film, Raquel and I both completed the Love Dare on our own.

The Love Dare touched me in many ways, but it was the concept of agape love that made the most impact. Who knew that a Greek snack dip could be *that* good? As a student of personal growth for more than twenty years, it was humbling to realize that I didn't have the slightest idea as to what love really is until I took the Love Dare. I learned that love isn't real love, or agape love, unless it is *unconditional.*

Unconditional love means just that, if I truly love someone, I love them *without condition.* Unconditional love is permanent and unchanging. It is unaffected by what someone else says or does. My love for my wife, children, parent, friend or anyone is unconditional when I love them *regardless of their behavior.*

This led me to reevaluate everything I thought I knew about love. I had to accept that, in many ways, my love *was* conditional. If someone I loved didn't meet my needs or expectations, my feelings and behavior would change. Even more convicting, I realized that I would occasionally do things for other people expecting something in return.

That isn't love, it's a transaction. When I love with strings attached, it can't be love because true love is selfless (not to be confused with selfish). Love is giving without condition or expectation of return. It is doing something for others out of the goodness of my heart. If it's anything less than that it may be a nice thing to do, but it is not and never will be love.

And here's the kicker: If I withhold love from someone because of something they did or said—it means I never really loved them to begin with. That's conditional love—love that's available only when certain conditions or behaviors are met. If someone I love fails to meet *my expectations,* the contract is voided, and my so-called love is withdrawn. That's not love—it's manipulation.

I've worked hard at learning how to love unconditionally—a process that has improved my relationships and helped me find that one of the keys to happiness isn't about getting what *I want*, but giving the people I love what *they need*. The more I devoted my life to others, the happier and more fulfilled I became.

This doesn't mean that I'm a doormat or that I allow my loved ones to do whatever they want. In fact, when I love unconditionally, I feel more comfortable setting boundaries or taking appropriate action *because* I'm doing it out of love—and not some selfish need or emotion.

I still marvel how one exchange during an ordinary lunch led me to this new understanding of love that continues to grow and bloom in my life. I've always believed in love. I just didn't understand it very well. But now I know if my thoughts, feelings, or actions are inconsistent with love—it's a red light on my dashboard telling me that I'm off course.

The path back is to remember that real love never makes exceptions. It can't. Love only knows love—and nothing else.

Dave Dabney
Bethesda, Maryland–May 2011

The Missing Link

You must take personal responsibility. You cannot change the circumstances, the seasons, or the wind, but you can change yourself.
—Jim Rohn

⚜

WHEN I STARTED DATING, one thing I never looked forward to was meeting my girlfriend's father. I was either avoided like the antichrist or interrogated like a criminal, but either way it was bad mojo for me. I'd get a look that seemed to say, *I don't like you. I'll never like you. And I hope this is the last time I ever see you.* I'd leave feeling like pond scum with my girlfriend blithely saying, "I think my dad really likes you." *Yeah*, I'd think, *I feel like I'm part of the family.*

I knew I wasn't exactly the catch of the year, but I didn't understand the depth of the animosity until I became a father/stepfather of three girls. What all dads know is that most teenage boys are afflicted with a condition informally known as hormonal possession, which is why father's live by a simple rule: *You're free to sow your wild oats, but not with my daughter.*

One thing I was certain of, however, is that any attempt on my part to influence their choice in boyfriends might only encourage a proliferation of the things I saw in my nightmares: body piercing, tattoos, ear gauges, random facial hair or pants worn around the knees. My only hope was to raise them in such a way that they would have the self-esteem to make decisions that reflected respect for self and others.

In Taylor's case, her mother gets the bulk of the credit for helping her develop into a preternaturally grounded, kind, and self-confident young woman. So I wasn't surprised when her first serious boyfriend didn't resemble anything like a character from a Tim Burton movie. When I first met Ian McLeod, he shook my hand and called me "Mr. Dwight." He was so polite and respectful I felt like I was Ward Cleaver.

A senior at St. Stephen's & St. Agnes high school, Ian was a starting guard for the basketball team, an honors student, and a piano player with spine-tingling talent. Over time our initial impressions of Ian were validated and our respect for him grew, but even with mounting evidence of high character, the wary stepfather in me still had him on my secret watch list.

After they had been dating for more than a year, Ian was home from college during Taylor's senior year at St. Stephens. It was a Saturday night and he planned to take Taylor to a jazz concert in Georgetown. Her mother was out of town, but had already given Taylor the green light to go.

I was reading upstairs when Ian walked in and asked to speak with me. He sat down, sighed, and said, "Mr. Dwight, I was going to take Taylor to a concert, but she has two exams on Monday and I don't think it's the right thing to do." Shaking his head, he added, "This is going to kill her, but I have to call this off. She needs to get some rest and study." I was agog.

It was such an improbable gesture that I started to question his motivations and his origins. *Who are you? What are you? Do you eat? Bleed? Are you even human?* The only explanation I could come up with was that he must be the missing link between our animal and civilized natures.

A short while later Taylor came upstairs, all dressed up with nowhere to go. "He wouldn't take me to the concert," she said in a soft, bewildered voice, "He said I needed to study. But I wanted him to take me out. I don't know what to do."

As for Ian McLeod, this was no act. Possessing thoughtfulness and maturity beyond his years, Ian consistently takes the needs and interests of others into account. He willingly accepts and embraces personal responsibility for his actions. During a dinner with Ian's parents, Brooke and Neil McLeod, Neil said that of everything they taught Ian, taking personal responsibility is the one thing that he stressed the most with him.

At his age, I was the living antonym of personal responsibility. Indeed, if I could identify one thing that has caused me more difficulty in any relationship, personal or professional, I'd say that it was my reluctance to take *full ownership* for my contribution to the problem. Why would I do that when there was always an explanation or someone else to blame?

I've resisted this truth and have failed many times to embrace it, but I can't outrun or escape it. *I am responsible* for everything in my life—and there is no other person, circumstance, or situation to blame. This is hard to accept, but when I do, it is empowering and liberating.

When I learned how to sincerely and humbly say, "That was my fault," or "I take full responsibility," whatever the issue was got resolved quickly or disappeared altogether. The level of trust in my relationships is proportionate to the degree of honesty I'm willing to share.

During the time I was writing this story, I was worried about a family situation while I was driving to my daughter's soccer game. When that happens I enter "Planet Art" and my awareness of what's happening around me drops precipitously. As I arrived at the entrance, a couple opened both doors and I walked right through them, unaware that they were opening the doors for themselves, not me.

"You're welcome, *asshole!*" he said in a harsh tone that told me he was ready to fight if I was. One of the things I like about "Planet Art" is that no one ever calls me that when I'm there. I was surprised and angry, but the instant I snapped back to reality I realized what

I did. I could argue that what he said was far more offensive than what I did, but that's irrelevant. The only thing I needed to concern myself with was *my behavior.*

I made a quick decision. I turned around caught up to the guy and said, "I just want to say that you're right and I'm sorry. I was upset about something and I wasn't paying attention." Now it was his turn to be surprised. "It's alright, man," he managed to say.

I was feeling pretty good about my verbal judo, but even better that a potentially negative or dangerous situation turned into a positive experience for me and the other person. What a different outcome it would've been if I focused on his behavior and didn't take responsibility for mine.

As for Taylor and Ian, after more than two years together, now at different colleges, they mutually decided it was time to be on their own for a while. It was hard on both of them, but because of the strength of their characters, they managed it with uncommon grace and mutual respect.

I am so proud of both of them—and humbled how much I can learn from the example these two young adults have set.

Ian and Taylor
Washington, DC–July 2010

We'll See

A half-truth is half-less than that.
—Unknown

——— ⚶ ———

HE MOMENT ALY got into the car I mentally braced myself for the sales pitch I knew was coming. It was the same pitch I had been hearing for months. Her desire for an iPhone had turned into an obsession. Every day it was a different tactic—and this day would be no different.

"Dad, did you know the iPhone has apps that can help me with my homework? I can access all the information I need, which means I'll get better grades. That's a good thing, right, Dad?" Before I could respond, she said in pleading, almost desperate tone, "But Dad, whatever you do, please don't say 'we'll see.' You can say anything else, but please don't say that!"

"Why don't you want me to say that, Aly?"

Grace jumped into the conversation to help her little sister, "Because she knows that 'we'll see' means no." I knew where this was headed, but I wasn't ready to concede the point yet. "Really?" I said.

"Yes," Grace continued. "We'll see is dad-speak for no. Now, 'maybe' isn't so bad, because maybe usually means yes, but 'we'll see' is definitely no, which really makes it a lie, doesn't it, Dad? She was on a roll—and then she went in for the kill: "Aren't you always telling us how important it is to tell the truth?"

There's nothing quite so humbling like being an author and speaker on the importance of integrity, only to be upbraided by my own child. There was no verbal magic or parental sleight of hand I could use to get out of this trap. I was busted and I had to come clean.

"You're right," I said. "The truth is, Aly, you're not going to get an iPhone this Christmas because our family plan is with Verizon and they don't have an iPhone. We'd have to pay a penalty to break our contract with Verizon in addition to paying more for a solo plan for your phone."

I explained to Aly that I didn't want to disappoint her, which was why I was saying "we'll see," instead of no. That explanation, however, didn't absolve me of my failure to communicate honestly.

One rule I strive to live by which goes by many different names, but carries the same meaning; walk the talk, practice what you preach, etc. I can't follow this rule, however, if I'm not aware that I'm breaking it. I'd been doing the parental shuffle with the girls, but I didn't realize how hypocritical it was until Grace called me on it.

This is where the rubber meets the road.

Like everyone I have blind spots, but the moment someone points it out to me, that's when I need to honor my commitment to think, speak and act with integrity. Or as my father so often advised me, "play it straight."

When I fail to communicate clearly and truthfully, I compound the problem I am trying to avoid. In the case of Aly's iPhone I did the "we'll see" two-step because I didn't want to disappoint her, but that only prolonged her agony and did nothing to improve our relationship.

This exchange reinforced a valuable lesson for me that it's either the truth or it's not. Every half-truth, evasion or indirect response plants a seed of doubt, which erodes trust and damages my relationships. The justification for it, no matter what the intention is, reflects poorly on my character. There is always a better way—and that is to always communicate as clearly, objectively and truthfully as I can.

As for Aly's phone, she did get the Fascinate, a pretty cool Samsung smartphone for Christmas. Three months later, of course, Verizon finally released its own version of the iPhone. Will Aly finally get one of those?

We'll see.

Alien Possession

Communication is to relationship what breathing is to life.
—VIRGINIA SATIR

THE LAST TIME IT HAPPENED I vowed it would never happen again. But a simple vow, I knew, would not be enough. I had made this mistake too many times. I had to go big. So I made a written contract with myself, signed it, declared it unbreakable, and read it every day for ninety days. After three months without incident, I smugly thought, *nailed another one, the Champion of Change does it again*. Satisfied, I put my pledge into the completed folder.

A few weeks later, Raquel was sharing some of her frustrations with me and that's when *it happened*. Without warning, the man alien inside me sprang into action, rapidly seizing control of my mind and body. He booted up the man computer, processed Raquel's data and swiftly produced a familiar solution:

WOMAN HAS PROBLEM. I AM A MAN. I MUST FIX IT. FIX THE PROBLEM. FIX THE PROBLEM. FIX THE PROBLEM.

Not so fast, man alien! I silently told him, *we have to think this through*. I asked Raquel for a minute, walked into my closet, closed the door and went mano e mano with my man alien. Our conversation went something like this:

"No, man alien, she doesn't want me to fix it. She just wants me to listen."

"Did she say that?"

"No, but..." I replied, weakening.

"Is it not perfectly clear that she has a problem?"

"Yes, but..."

"And don't you have the solution?"

"Yes, but I made a vow..."

"Let me break it down for you. She is upset. She has a problem and you have the solution. If you love her, go out there and fix her problem. She *wants* you to fix it. She *needs* you to fix it. You are a man. This is what you do."

I could not dispute man alien's flawless logic. This time is different, I rationalized. She *really does* want me to fix it! Thus emboldened, I walked into the bedroom and told Raquel what she needed to do. As I was talking, her face fell like a brick in a pond. My man alien was confused; unable to understand what was happening. *Didn't I have the perfect solution? Why is she not rejoicing and speaking words of undying gratitude for having such a brilliant man in her life?*

She paused and I knew it was coming, the thing I dreaded. I would've done anything to stop it, to turn back the hands of time, but it was too late. The damage was done. I did it again. In a soft voice brimming with disbelief, disappointment and hurt, she delivered the verdict, "I didn't want advice. I just wanted you to listen."

Ahhhhh! You @##! I told you this would happen, man alien*, I silently screamed, as he feebly shrunk back into the cave of my subconscious, leaving me to face the consequences alone. I was so desperate for a way out that I considered telling her the truth. *Raquel, please let me explain. It wasn't me! It was my man alien. I tried to stop him, but he was too strong.* But as much as I wanted to rely on the alien possession defense, it's a bit thin and arguably psychotic.

The truth was that I had blown it. Again. I felt terrible that I had broken my pledge to honor and respect Raquel by keeping my ears open and my mouth shut, but this experience renewed my determination to understand why this happened and to prevent it from ever happening again. The question that vexed me was: How I can *know* what I should do and yet still make the same mistake?

There really are two forces at work within me and it *is* a lot like alien possession. One force is the thoughts, ideas and beliefs formed by the influences of my family, culture, and the environment in which I was raised. This is my alien. The other force is the thoughts, ideas and beliefs that I've learned through books, other people, and life experiences. This is the person I'm striving to become, independent of my past influences.

My brain is programmed to respond to perceived problems by seeking a solution. Like many men, this is how I am wired. There's nothing right or wrong about this, but conflict is inevitable when my alien's need for solving meets Raquel's need to be heard.

In the past, I was clueless as to why we'd have these misunderstandings. All I knew is that her feelings were hurt, I was frustrated and confused and we'd keep having the same disagreements over and over again with no resolution in sight. I knew that the only path out was a full understanding as to why I couldn't keep my promise to Raquel.

The shocking truth was that despite all of the positive changes I had made in my life, my alien was still controlling far too many of my thoughts, emotions, and actions. He is one tough, resilient hombre. But so am I. One of us had to go—and it wasn't going to me. I had to do more than win battles in the bedroom closet. I had to kill him.

The difference this time was that I knew how to do it and I was certain I could. All I had to do was destroy the source of his power, which he derives from making decisions without my conscious awareness. His game is to work in the shadows of my mind like a silent assassin, controlling my reactions, pushing my buttons, and sabotaging my relationships. My alien knows this, which is why exposure and logic are the things he fears the most.

And that's exactly what I gave him. Every time I felt myself starting to react according to an old pattern, I took a time out and had a little talk with my alien.

"Oh, hello man alien. I know what you're up to and I know what you want to do."

"But listen…"

"No, shut your alien pie hole and *you* listen. I'm onto you and I'm calling my own shots from now on."

Is this schizophrenia? Perhaps, but it works. Light is to the man alien what water is to the Wicked Witch of the West. Every time I call him out he grows weaker and I grow stronger. By repeatedly making the decisions that I want to make, I'm forming a new habit that is stronger than the alien.

It's been a year since I took this stand and I've kept my promise to Raquel. And now that I've developed a habit of making my own decisions, my man alien isn't dead but he's substantially less influential. Ironically, I have to credit his expertise in solution finding that brought me to this place. Something I'm not sure he would have gone along with had he known it would result in his destruction.

With Raquel
Alexandria, Virginia–December 2010

Truly Gifted

Don't die with the music still in you.
—Dr. Wayne Dyer

As I watched Taylor perform in St. Stephen's rendition of *Pippen* during her senior year in high school, I felt like I was listening to the voice of an angel. I thought about how much beauty and talent there is within every one of us, and what a Chicago pastor once said in a eulogy, "The saddest thing isn't the death of the person, but the death of his dreams."

I've always had a dream of being able to sing in front of a crowd. But unlike Taylor, I have no such gift. A friend once compared my singing to the sound of a sick frog in bondage. When I was a waiter after college, I hid in the kitchen when it was time to sing the group birthday song. The general manager got wise to my act and one evening he tracked me down and told me I had to sing. "Okay," I said. "You're the boss."

I opened up at full volume. My voice had the effect of an experimental Pentagon weapon tested for the first time on unsuspecting subjects—every conversation in that packed restaurant stopped cold as if their vocal chords had been paralyzed. The other waiters just looked at me, their faces a mixture of shock and disbelief.

That was more than twenty-five years ago, and as my gift to the world I have never sung publicly since. I have other gifts, but the challenge for me has been figuring out exactly what they are. One of my mistakes has been to compare myself to others, a depressing exercise because I can always find someone who does it better.

When I read great books I feel inspired by the author's talent, but I often feel depressed because my writing seems weak by comparison. *Who am I kidding?* I'd think. *I'm not an author. I'm a charlatan.* And when people would enthusiastically tell me that they love my writing I'd think, *did you read the same thing I did?*

This isn't exclusively my negative self-perception. I reviewed each story for the book you're reading at least thirty times before I submitted it to my editor. When she returned my edited manuscript it looked like a literary massacre—there were at least *fourteen hundred* corrections. Apparently I have issues with excessive commas, capitalization, verb agreement, and overstatement (Author's note: she did not review this paragraph prior to publication. Any errors are my own).

Fortunately, in contradistinction to this shortcoming, people have told me about changes they've made in their lives because of something that I said or wrote; how they pursued their dreams, started a new business, improved their relationships or found peace in some area of their life. What I've heard most often is that they can relate to my honesty—and that it helps to know that we share some of the same struggles, thoughts and feelings.

Interestingly, I had a difficult time relating to what others shared with me about my work. I felt uncomfortable and embarrassed. As I struggled to understand why that was I realized that my own self-doubt was getting in the way of an important discovery—what they were telling me *is* my gift!

It's not my writing talents, speaking style or even the message itself—none of which is new, groundbreaking, or even that original—it's my willingness to share my deepest thoughts, feelings, fears, and vulnerabilities. Sharing the moments of my life with all of the honesty, self-awareness and insight that I can possibly bring to them is the gift that is uniquely mine.

I've also accepted that it's the *quality* of the gift, not the *quantity* that matters. If I'm only really good at *one thing*—then developing and perfecting that gift is what I'm here to do. This was a reassuring discovery because I'm married to a woman who is so multi-talented that if I spent too much time comparing myself to her I might lose my incentive for living.

Gifts, of course, are meant to be shared. I believe that my life's purpose is to continue to develop and share my gift to the full extent of my ability. My own growth in this area helps me appreciate, admire, and enjoy the gifts of others, especially Raquel, Taylor, Grace and Aly—who are the greatest gifts in my life.

Taylor, right, performing at St. Stephen's & St. Agnes
Alexandria, Virginia–April 2010

Her Corner of the World

If you are what you should be, you will set the world on fire.
—St. Catherine of Siena

———— ⚜ ————

"DO YOU HAVE ANY IDEA how good your sister is?" Janet Durgin, the head of Sonoma Academy, asked me at Ellie's fiftieth birthday party.

I didn't know what to say, except, "I have a glimpse of that."

"Let me give you more than a glimpse," she said. "She is the heart and soul of our school. She is loved, revered, and respected by the students, the faculty and the board of directors." And she concluded with this clock-stopping compliment, "Ellie *is* Sonoma Academy."

I was embarrassed. I had just learned from someone I had never met before that my sister was the educational equivalent of a rock star. I knew she was outgoing and smart, but the "heart and soul of the entire school?" Clueless.

As I wondered why that was I realized that Ellie never talks about herself or her accomplishments—a sign of greatness in its own right. Ellie spends the moments of her life shaping and influencing young men and women to become something greater than what they are. There are no headlines, awards or trumpets for Ellie, only the satisfaction of knowing that she's doing meaningful work that makes a difference.

Her work is a wonderful illustration of someone who quietly goes about tending to her little corner of the world. It's an inspiring reminder that's what I need to do in my own work. At times I feel discouraged because I feel I'm not making enough of an impact or that my reach isn't big enough—a nagging feeling that somehow I'm always falling short.

Ellie helps me see that the only thing I can do is to give my best to everyone I touch in my life. The work itself isn't the important thing, what's important is to do everything I can to serve, influence or touch everyone in my little corner of the world. Every moment of every day is a new opportunity to do that.

My part in changing the world involves every interaction of the day whether it's doing something for my children, parents, friends, co-workers, customers or even strangers. It could be as big as a mission trip or as small as buying someone a cup of coffee. Even one smile or kind gesture makes a difference.

The way to change the world is one moment at a time.

It's said that if we positively influence the life of one person, then we are making a difference in thousands of lives downstream. When I think of the hundreds of students Ellie touches every year, she's creating a ripple effect that will ultimately touch the lives of millions.

I feel hopeful for our future knowing there are so many educators like Ellie helping to motivate and teach our children. And I feel inspired that I'm going to help make a difference today by doing the best I can in my little corner of the world. When that happens, changing the world doesn't feel so big or impossible after all.

Ellie with her daughter Reilly
New York City–July 2010
Photo: Laura Dwight Photography

A Mother's Love

A mother's love for her child is like nothing else in the world.
—Agatha Christie

I HAD A DREAM THAT my father and his wife were being tortured by the Taliban with a power drill in their Beacon Hill apartment. This presents some interesting questions as to exactly what the Taliban could extract from them except, perhaps, their Boston Red Sox season tickets, but it would take more than a power drill to separate them from my father. And aside from whatever pathology this might indicate for me, the really disturbing thing is that I woke up in a cold sweat at three a.m. to the *sound of a power drill* downstairs.

As my brain struggled to shake off sleep, I knew that Raquel and I were alone that night and she was still in bed (at least I thought she was), which meant something really was going on downstairs. I didn't like the odds of taking on the Taliban in my underwear, but they were torturing my parents so it appeared that the situation called for a heroic gesture, even a suicidal one.

As I stumbled down the stairs, my fuzzy, adrenaline-flooded brain struggled to make sense of the situation. *For starters*, I thought, *I don't think my parents are here. Secondly, although the drilling sound is real, I don't hear any screaming, which is weird because I'd be screaming like a girl on a roller coaster. Thirdly,* as I got closer, *the power drill started sounding an awful lot like a kitchen appliance.*

As I turned the corner from the hallway to confront the threat, I discovered that it wasn't a terrorist with a power drill, or even Colonel Mustard with a knife; it was Raquel, the pastry chef, in the kitchen with an electric mixer. "Hi, honey," she said with alacrity. "I couldn't sleep and I've been worried about the girls so I thought I'd make a cake for them."

Now, a part of me wanted to laugh (thinking, *oh, that's why there wasn't any screaming, flour doesn't have any nerve endings*), another part of me wanted to hug her, but mostly I was really irritated and desperately wanted to unleash the cacophony of thoughts in my mind such as, *it's really sweet what you're doing and all, but at three a.m. in the $%#@ morning? Oh, and by the way,* THANK YOU *for insisting I sell my gun. I can't tell you how comforting it was to take on the Taliban unarmed and practically naked!*

But instead of unleashing this verbal artillery, I didn't say anything. I sat down, partly because I was too stunned by the turn of events to do anything else, but primarily because I made a decision a long time ago to try and never say anything when I am upset, to *think before I speak.* I don't always succeed, but I did this time.

I listened while Raquel talked about our daughters; the challenges they were facing this fall, and how proud she was of them, but that she was worried and felt powerless to help them. "So when I woke up at two-thirty this morning," she said. "I realized I can only do so much with their homework and the drama they experience with their friends and school, but maybe I can make things easier if I have something special when they come home, which is why I'm baking this cake."

It was a cake that Aly had been talking about for weeks and it was fantastically complicated to prepare; three layers, different icings in the middle and on the top. And the entire time she was talking, she continued chopping pecans, making icing, beating flour, putting on a clinic in multi-tasking that I'd swear was impossible if I weren't seeing it with my own eyes. I made a mental note to continue buying pre-made bakery goods.

After my brain rebooted later that day, I had a chance to reflect on everything Raquel had shared with me. I was awed by the depth and power of her love for Taylor, Grace, and Aly. It wasn't just special, it was sacred. I called her at work to tell her how much I appreciated the love she has for our daughters—and how the cake she made was such a beautiful expression of that love. I apologized for not saying anything at the time, but she told me how glad she was that I listened because she just needed to talk.

When she said that I realized what a different outcome there would have been if I had lashed out at her. I would never have had the privilege of seeing her deep love for our daughters, and I would've missed the chance to deepen and strengthen our relationship too. And if I had criticized her, I would've lost more than a special moment; I would've trampled her feelings, caused her to retreat emotionally, and likely diminished our ability to share moments like that in the future.

It was a lightning bolt reminder on the power of my choices. Any given moment is a fork in the road with two diametrically different outcomes—one choice leads to deeper appreciation, understanding, and unity while the other leads to hurt, resentment, and separation. It's an enduring reminder, when in doubt, to always keep my mouth shut and my ears open.

I don't always succeed at this, but I'm glad I did this time. Instead of an unhappy outcome, not only did I save my parents from the Taliban, but I had the privilege to see and experience something truly special—the depth of a mother's love. And because we shared that moment, we were both able to share in another one that night when Aly's face lit up seeing that big, beautiful cake on the kitchen counter as she exclaimed with delight, "Raquel, you made the cake!"

Yes, she certainly did.

Taylor, Aly, the Cake, Raquel/Mom and Grace
Alexandria, Virginia–September 2010

Keeping the Peace

Be content with what you have, rejoice in the way things are. When you realize there is nothing lacking, the whole world belongs to you.
—LAO TZU

—+—❧—+—

THERE HAVE BEEN MOMENTS in my life that are so fixed in my mind I can recall almost every detail and emotion as if it happened yesterday. I had one of those moments this October as I gazed out at the Shenandoah Valley in Virginia from the highest point on Skyline Drive. In that moment, I was so consumed by its peace and beauty that I couldn't ever imagine feeling any other way.

But at the same time, I knew our vacation would end soon and I would be back in the world where the pace and challenges of daily life would invariably take this peace away. *Why is that?* I wondered. And could I change it? Could I bring this peace with me and keep it, regardless of life's challenges? I resolved to try.

When I got back home I put my resolution into action. I don't like to brag, but I nailed it. Compared to me, the Buddha was a drama queen. When it came to enlightenment, Satori or levitation, the Dalai Lama would soon be seeking my advice. I was the king of calm, the paragon of peace.

But a funny thing happened on the way to my coronation as the greatest spiritual master since Gandhi. I received a few buzz-killing emails, encountered a major schedule change, found a big gap in our college funds and one of my daughters had an epic meltdown. Familiar feelings of worry and anxiety, which I thought I had left behind, came roaring back. The peace of the Shenandoah Valley worked magic… *for nearly two whole days.*

But this time, there was a difference. Although I lost the peace I had been enjoying, I was aware of what was happening and *why* it was happening. I was able to put distance between myself and my circumstances and maintain perspective. I didn't get sucked into the drama.

Before I got too worked up about things, my thoughts traveled back to that quiet moment in the Virginia mountains and I thought about something I read there that hit me like a freight train at full speed. If I have food, clothing, and shelter then I have everything I *need*. It was so simple, yet so powerful. I could see, experience, and embrace the full truth of it.

Food, clothing and shelter are the only things in my life that can correctly be described as a need and having those three things alone is a blessing and cause for gratitude and celebration. Anything else that I have or want in my life is an added blessing, but it is not, and never will be a need.

I thought about the things that disturb my peace of mind like my retirement account performance, paying for three college educations, where we're going to live next year (my wife's in the Navy), balancing family schedules, etc.—and realized they are all part of my life situation, but none of them are actual needs.

When I faced my first post-vacation crisis, I realized that life's challenges rarely present themselves in a measured, orderly way. They tend to come in bunches, which can feel chaotic and overwhelming. But that, of course, is just my perception. Things that seem so important, so big, are just part of the ebb and flow of life—and not one of them has any bearing on what I need or what truly matters.

The worries and stress in my life is due to my perception of it. I am thankful for everything in my life, but I also keep a healthy respect for the impermanence of it all. If I worry about something, I ask myself: What is missing? The honest answer is nothing.

If I lost everything I have materially and found myself in a one-room apartment with just enough food and clothing to survive, could I still be happy? The answer is a resounding, unqualified yes. I am one of the luckiest people on earth. And I recall that quiet, magic moment in the Shenandoah Mountains, and realize that just being alive on this day is the greatest blessing I could ever ask for. I lack nothing.

I have everything I need.

Me on Skyline Drive
Shenandoah Valley, Virginia–October 2010

It's Not Personal

Don't take anything personally.
—Don Miguel Ruiz

WHENEVER MY OPINION of myself starts to get ahead of my pursuit of humility, I don't need a slap in the face—I just need a few minutes with my children. During the past few months, my ego has been put in check with surgical precision. Here is a sample of a few conversations:

Aly was away at summer camp and asked me to get her specific books from her eighth grade summer reading list. They didn't have one of the ones she wanted at the bookstore, so I picked *Manhunt* from the list, a book about the hunt for John Wilkes Booth, secretly hoping it might lead her to share my passion for history. And in the interest of full disclosure, I wanted to read it, too. When I gave her the book, she dropped it like it was burning her fingers:

"Dad, *whyyyyy* did you get me *Manhunt?*"

"It's an exciting story; I think you'll really like it."

"Ugh," Aly groaned.

"I thought we could bond?"

"I don't want to bond with you."

A few weeks later, as we were leaving the house, I noticed we were wearing the same colors, light khaki shorts and blue shirts:

"Hey Aly, look, we're wearing the same clothes."

"Oh, no, Dad!!"

"Don't you think it's cool?"

"I'm going to change *right now*," Aly yelled as she stormed away.

I was driving to pick Grace up after she attended a summer program for Johnson & Wales University in Providence, Rhode Island. I was heading to the celebration breakfast for parents and students when Grace sent me the following text:

"Dad, when are you getting here?"

"I'm just a few minutes away!" I replied, excited that she wants to see me.

"Dad, please don't take this the wrong way, but would you *not* sit with me?"

And for three years, Taylor ignored my requests to "friend her" on Facebook. It became a running joke in our family that I played along with, but in all honesty it hurt my feelings. Last week my wife was giving me an update on her morning, saving the killing blow for last, and smugly declared, "Oh, and Taylor friended me on Facebook."

These moments remind me to live the wisdom shared by Don Miguel Ruiz in his book, *The Four Agreements*, to not take anything personally. If ever the expression easier said than done had application, it's with this. When someone close to me like my wife, parent, sibling or child, does or says something that hurts, how can I *not* take it personally?

But if I put my feelings on hold and think, it doesn't take long for me to drink Ruiz's ancient Toltec wisdom and realize that he's right—nothing *is* personal—it just *feels* personal. Whatever someone else says or does belongs entirely to them. If I take it personally, I'm turning it into something about *me*. If I do that, I'm *deciding* to make it personal. And if I'm being brutally honest with myself, it's a self-centered way of looking at it.

This wisdom applies to everyone and every situation without exception.

If someone gives me a nasty look, sends me a harsh email, doesn't smile, won't return my phone calls, cuts me off from my turn lane, gives me the finger, insults my mother or gets into my face and screams at full volume with spit flying from their mouth, that I am the ugliest, fattest most pathetic person they have ever seen in their life…none of it is personal. Not even a little, tiny bit.

If I take something personally, it means that whatever the other person did or said triggered something in me. The only way it could upset me is if I agree with it. If I don't believe that about myself, then those comments would have no effect. Those comments aren't about me; they are a projection of that person's own self-image.

One of the rules I work to live by in relationships is that whatever someone else says or does belongs to them and whatever I say or do belongs to me. Each of us has one hundred percent ownership of our actions and not even one percent of the other person's stuff belongs to me. They own their stuff and I own my stuff. And the only thing I need to concern myself with is my stuff.

So when Grace sent me the text asking me not to sit with her, I sent her a text back, "Who is *this?*" Missing the joke, she texted back, "Dad, it's ME, Grace." Adding, "It's okay, you can sit with me." And Aly doesn't mind being identified with me; she's just thirteen and is embarrassed to be publicly associated with me right now. And as for Taylor, she's now my Facebook friend as I knew one day she would be. I just had to be patient…and not take it personally.

Taylor, Grace, me and Aly
Boston, Massachusetts–June 2011

A Change of Venue

Communication works for those who work at it.
—JOHN POWELL

━━◆━━

THE BEST CONVERSATIONS I've had rarely occur where I spend most of my time. It happened again during a hike with Grace and Aly on Maryland Heights, across the river from Harpers Ferry, West Virginia. The only dialogue we had on the way up consisted of a lot of huffing and puffing, punctuated by occasional, "How much further?" questions. But when we got to the top, the view was so breathtaking that even my teenagers were touched by its beauty.

On the way back down, Aly started talking about a book she'd been reading about the Holocaust, which prompted Grace to share her thoughts on the subject. I was impressed with their knowledge and understanding of the events—but I was especially gratified by the sensitivity, empathy, and compassion they had for the victims.

It was the kind of conversation that parents live for.

I felt privileged to have this moment with girls who will be following their older sister to college faster than I can fathom. These are the moments that I treasure and value, when I know that everything we've done or sacrificed for them has been worth it. It's a feeling of joy, pride and satisfaction that brings out the richness, wonder and magic of life.

It's a karmic mind-bender to think that this moment would have never happened if I didn't encourage them to go hiking with me that day. When it comes to productive conversations with teenage girls, I was batting well below .200 so I enlisted the help of a family therapist and coach, Dr. Beverly Celotta, who said if I wanted their cooperation I should speak in terms of how much I would personally appreciate their help.

The night before the hike I told the girls how much I would love it if they would go hiking with me, but that we'd have to get up early. And to my amazement—they both signed on without complaint. While this may seem like shameless manipulation, I meant every word of it. Thank you Dr. Bev.

It's amazing what a change in venue can do for a relationship. There is something magical about a neutral place. It liberates me from the trappings and pressures of daily life and frees up precious mental space and energy to be with the other person.

I love our home, but it also represents work. There's always some kind of mental pressure that something needs to be done. It's difficult to feel relaxed and focused when I'm mentally conflicted and it's especially challenging to have a quality conversation with all of that other static buzzing in my head. On our hike, just leaving the iPods and cell phones in the car freed up mental space and allowed conversation to flow.

After church on Sunday mornings my wife and I cherish our weekly trip to Starbucks. It's our special time to catch up, reconnect, or just simply be with each other. We're five minutes from home, but it could well be five hundred miles. In that comfortable, neutral place, we can listen, understand and work through anything that needs our attention.

If I'm dealing with a challenging work or personal situation, the first thing I do is look for a change of venue. Whenever possible, I break away and spend time outdoors. Just going for a walk, sitting on a bench or spending a few minutes in nature frees my mind to think constructively and creatively.

It's a simple little change that makes a big difference.

Grace, me and Aly
Overlooking Harper's Ferry, West Virginia–April 2010

Less is More

Simplify, simplify, simplify.
—Henry David Thoreau

—·⊹※⊹·—

R AQUEL AND I TRIED an experiment that was so risky and unpre-
dictable that even the most reckless scientist might be reluctant
to undertake it. We wondered what would happen if we took away
all technology from four teenage girls, including cell phones, iPods,
laptops and Facebook—and then put them to work digging ditches
every day for a week in a tropical climate in July.

Taylor, Grace, Aly and our niece, Lauren, all willingly agreed to
go, but we still had no idea how they would react to the experience
of replacing our family vacation with a mission trip to Banica, an
extremely impoverished community in the Dominican Republic on
the Haitian border. During the mission Raquel and I were impressed
with how hard they worked and how well they connected with the
Dominican children, but given all of the hardships, we were still
wondering what the final verdict might be.

As the bus was pulling away from Banica for the trip home, we
didn't have to wait long for our answer. Aly spun around in her seat,
locked her eyes on mine and said in a voice brimming with life-or-
death intensity, "Dad, we need to go back to Banica."

"I know, honey, we'll go back next year," I replied with one of my lamer parental responses.

"No, Dad, you're *not* getting it. We need to turn the bus around and go back, *right now.*" At a rest stop three hours later, we even caught Aly and Lauren scheming to hitch a ride back to Banica.

During our week there they endured physical work, long hours, heat, mosquitoes, basic food, no air conditioning, and little down-time—and I've never seen them happier. In the evening hours they spent time with kids from Banica sharing and exchanging games, dances and stories. Aly and Lauren taught the Dominican girls the "Happy Feet Dance," which I imagine is still being practiced there.

They developed an easy, natural connection despite coming from different worlds, speaking different languages and considering the primitive conditions in Banica, a different time in history. I've always believed in the equality of people of all races, cultures, and circumstances but this experience proved it to me in a way that no book or classroom ever could.

My initial fear was that our girls would never forgive me, but it turned out to be one of the most enjoyable and fulfilling experiences of their lives. It's inspired me to reevaluate everything I know about happiness. It illuminates the ancient and biblical wisdom that less is more. This was validated in even greater depth through our experience with the people we came to serve.

Our mission was to build outdoor latrines for families who have never had bathroom facilities. Our family comprised six of the eighteen missionaries from a group called Commissioned by Christ who traveled to Banica to work with Dominican laborers to construct outdoor latrines. In the greater Banica area more than fifty percent of the 15,000 Dominicans lack basic bathroom facilities.

The families we served lived in huts built with sticks, mud, and straw roofs so primitive they could pass for housing built five thousand years ago. They had no furniture or household items of any kind, save one cast-iron pot they used to cook communal meals that they all shared with one spoon. They slept on dirt floors with no sheets or blankets.

Despite these conditions, the people of Banica were more relaxed, peaceful and authentic without material things, including things we would normally consider basic, essential comforts. Coming from the developed world, I struggled to make sense of this apparent contradiction. *How can they be so happy in these conditions?*

This doesn't mean that the people of Banica are problem free, far from it. Extreme poverty is the root cause of deplorable situations, including domestic abuse and fathers who essentially sell their young daughters to wealthier men in exchange for basic necessities. But that's what makes the contrast even more astonishing. Even under those circumstances the Dominicans exhibited a natural kindness and easy peace far greater than my own.

My return to our world put an exclamation point on the experience. I was in Target the day after coming home when I noticed no one was smiling. Indeed, no one looked even remotely happy. We have an abundance of material possessions but outwardly appear miserable. In their world, they have nothing and outwardly seem happy.

Later that night I read something so timely and relevant it felt like it was some kind of cosmic special delivery just for me. In an article about Mother Teresa, the author wrote that it was her belief that the spiritual poverty of the developed world was *a far more serious problem* than the material poverty of the undeveloped world. This was an epiphany on steroids. I felt like shouting up to Heaven, "I got it. Thank you!"

The take away for me wasn't as dramatic as taking a vow of poverty or eschewing all material possessions, but a confirmation that my possessions have *absolutely nothing* to do with contentment, peace or happiness. And that all the stuff in my life, instead of making me happier, tends to clutter it up. It reminds me of something that Henry David Thoreau wrote more than 150 years ago. He said that our lives are "frittered away in details" and that the secret to life is to, "simplify, simplify, simplify."

I don't have the option of retreating to Walden Pond, but I can make choices on what's important in my life by identifying and reducing the things that distract and divide my attention. The simpler I can make my life, the more room I have for focusing on what matters: my faith, my relationships and my family. When I do that, I am truly happy. I will always be grateful to the people of Banica for giving me so much more than I gave to them.

Less is indeed more.

Aly, Lauren, Grace and Taylor
Banica, Dominican Republic–July 2010

Banica's Angels

Lower is Higher

No man is an island entire of itself; every man
is a piece of the continent, a part of the main.
—JOHN DONNE

DIGGING A TEN-FOOT-DEEP latrine in a remote corner of the world would seem an unlikely place to discover an important truth. But that one act of service helped me understand that giving everything I had to give to someone else, with no thought or expectation of getting anything in return, is one of the most important things I can do with my life.

For more than twenty years I had been reading and reflecting on this truth through philosophers and scripture, and I always felt inspired by it, but I could never quite seem to live it. When we finished building our latrine during our mission trip in the Dominican Republic, however, I had a new appreciation for what living a life of purpose really means.

The Dominican family who we built an outhouse for had been living without a bathroom for their entire lives. After four days of physically grueling, dirty work we knocked on the door of their mud and straw hut and invited them to see the finished product. The look of wonder and joy on their faces was the greatest compensation for anything I have ever done in my life.

That moment will stay with me forever and I wouldn't trade it for anything, but the real magic of the experience was that I didn't need it. I would have been just as fulfilled doing the work in complete anonymity with no recognition or acknowledgement of any kind. That was the difference. That's how I knew I had found what I've been searching for.

I don't think it was an accident that the path to this truth began in a hole that would soon become someone's bathroom. It was a perfect reminder that I started as dust and will end as dust, just like the people I worked with and the people we came to serve. We are all, truly interconnected.

Any act of service, no matter how small, elevates everyone involved. By digging deeper into that hole, I was able to achieve greater separation from the ego-based self I left behind and found an indescribable feeling of giving my heart, mind, body and spirit in service to someone in need. The lower I went, the higher I rose.

How fitting it was that only when I had been stripped of most everything material in my life—completely disconnected from my world of technology, comfort, and excess—was I able to see the truth of life in a way I never had before. By getting down into the dirt I found a path up to a world of meaning, fulfillment, purpose and joy that transcended anything I had ever experienced. Now that's happiness!

I've finally come to understand what all the great writers, teachers, and philosophers such as Socrates, Jesus, Gandhi or Mother Teresa have been trying to tell me. I never disagreed with them, of course, but I just couldn't grasp it until I experienced it for myself. And now that I have, I feel like I'm on a mission trip every day, ready to love and serve others to the very best of my ability.

Me and Joe Pianese
Banica, Dominican Republic–July 2010

The Blind Side

You can't escape from a prison if you don't know you're in one.
—Unknown

WHEN I WAS IN MY TWENTIES, I was an intellectual giant. I hadn't even been to medical school, for instance, but I knew everything there was to know about ADHD. "Look at these kids," I'd say to anyone who cared to listen. "They're hyper because they eat too much sugar, and watch too many video games while their parents are asleep at the wheel." I thought it was a crime to medicate kids for it and that ADHD wasn't really an illness, but a conspiracy between psychiatrists and drug companies.

So when my daughter Grace was diagnosed with ADHD after a comprehensive evaluation when she was five years old, I dismissed it. It was a simple process of elimination. We gave her reasonably healthy food, her video intake was limited to Disney movies and, of course, my parenting couldn't possibly be to blame. I had all the answers.

But there was something else going on with me that I never shared with anyone, not even Raquel; I secretly worried that I was intellectually impaired or brain damaged in some way. I didn't process things, learn or interact socially the way other "normal" people seemed to. I needed Cliff Notes for conversations.

Even if jokes were repeated three times, I'd still be trying to figure it out while everyone else was having paroxysms on the floor. I sometimes joined in with a fake, self-conscious laugh that screamed that I had no idea why I was laughing. I wondered constantly, *what is wrong with me?*

I could stay with conversations for five minutes on a good day before my mind would drift away even though I did everything in my power to will it not to. When I was in meetings where I had to sustain my attention for long periods of time, I resorted to masochism. I'd slide my hand under my thigh to give myself a "horse bite," grabbing and squeezing my flesh as hard as possible, inflicting enough pain to help me focus for a few more minutes.

As I grew older, I experienced increasingly wide swings in my physical and mental energy throughout the day. I would get so mentally drained sometimes that I took naps not because I wanted to, but because I had to. When I was in a low cycle, just *thinking* about basic things took great effort. In social situations, especially at night, I was constantly running a few sentences behind.

I couldn't bring myself to talk about what I was going through with anyone because it felt like I was admitting to a weakness that I should've been able to control. So I self-treated myself through a fanatical commitment to exercise, diet, prayer and meditation. I even eliminated almost all simple sugar and alcohol, which improved things, but it did not cure me.

I was feeling desperate because I couldn't think of anything else I could do. I'd emptied the playbook and I was still struggling. Every day I felt like I was pushing a huge bolder up hill in the rain—and no matter what I did to get stronger, I kept sliding backward. About this time Grace received a second diagnosis of ADHD. And when her doctor spoke of the "strong genetic connection," I couldn't rationalize this away anymore.

As I reviewed my daughter's report I wasn't just reading about her—I was reading about *me*. I took an online self-test and this is the message I received at the end. YOUR ADHD QUIZ SAYS:

SERIOUS ADHD LIKELY!

*You should not take this as a diagnosis of any sort, or a recommendation for treatment. However, it would be advisable and likely beneficial for you to seek further diagnosis from a trained mental health professional **immediately.***

The only thing missing from that message were the sirens, flashing lights and big, muscle-bound male nurses wielding syringes. When I told Raquel about my "discovery" she gave me a look that said, "And this is news, how?" Apparently my ADHD for anyone who had knowledge or experience with it wasn't exactly a secret. It took more than half my life to finally recognize, admit, and accept the truth that I had an illness.

I realized that everything I previously believed about ADHD was wrong. It is not an environmentally-created condition. It's a real disability. ADHD is essentially an imbalance in mental functioning caused by reduced blood flow to the brain, which explains my inconsistent attention and mental energy drains. It also explained the hyperactivity. Sitting still feels uncomfortable because I'm relying on an under-powered brain, so my body would overcompensate with a powerful drive to move around.

For the first time in my life, all these things I had been struggling with started making sense. I was so relieved!

I'd devoted my life to the benefits of uncovering the truth and here I was getting the lesson of a lifetime on denial. Denial is the most insidious and inconceivably destructive force in my life. I suffered with a condition for the majority of my life because I had "created" a defense system designed to keep me from seeing the truth.

So instead of getting help I tried to go it alone with a strategy that helped, but would never succeed. That's why I'm more certain than ever that one of the most important things I can do is *look*. If I can't take this first step, I condemn myself to a life of ignorance and stagnation—I will never learn, change or grow.

My inability to see and acknowledge my illness reinforced the value of finding my blind spots before they find me. When I'm successful in doing this, I avoid being blindsided by others and I'm able to accelerate my learning, growth and potential. Every time I strip away my defenses and look at the truth, I move out of the shadows and into a brighter world.

There is no cure for ADHD. It is a condition that I will have every day for the rest of my life. I can't conquer it and I can't get rid of it, but I do take medicine daily and the results border on miraculous. It's still a struggle and I have to monitor my mental and physical state every day. But now that I can say, without shame or embarrassment that I have ADHD. I am no longer living my life fighting an unknown enemy.

I am free.

Lights Out

Everything we possess that is not necessary for life or happiness becomes a burden, and scarcely a day passes that we do not add to it.
—ROBERT BRAULT

——— ═╪═ ———

I WENT TO BED DURING a power outage recently and was enjoying a coma-like sleep until the power came back on. As every electronic device in our home suddenly jolted back to life, I woke up with my heart pounding. When I opened my eyes I felt like I was in a planetarium. I had never consciously noticed that we have more than a dozen lights emanating from a carnival of technology: TV, cable box, sound system, smoke detector, kindles, cell phones, home phones, etc.

It was the contrast that shocked me. During the power outage our home was dark, quiet and peaceful and I was enjoying one of the best sleeps in memory. When the electricity came back on and everything roared back to life, I realized just how much technology has enveloped my life. Sure, it's great, but should it be something that interferes with a good night's rest? That's not right.

I questioned technology in my life beyond the bedroom and realized just how detrimental it can be on so many different levels. From the minute I wake up to check my emails to the time I go to bed, I'm under a steady technological assault. My mind is constantly having to switch gears between texts, emails, phone calls, or internet surfing. And sometimes at night I'm using my laptop, cell phone and watching TV at the same time along with everyone else in my family.

It's said that our minds can only focus on one thing at a time. Since the only things I have of value are the moments of my life, I realized that these different technologies were taking the moments of my life and splitting them into pieces. I was living a divided life—never fully experiencing or appreciating any moment without being zapped this way or that.

During a talk about technology someone once said that we are exposed to one million bits of data every day and that exposure doubles every three years. What does that mean? I have no idea, but I do know what it's doing to my life. It's making me nuts. And since my foundation was a bit shaky to begin with, this wasn't a good thing.

But the most disturbing consequence of all this stimulation was that it was diminishing my ability to fulfill the most important function in my life—to *think*. I saw it as a simple formula: more technology, less thinking. Any contributions of value that I've made have been the product of creative thought, which only flows when I'm focused. And the things that truly matter: beauty, truth, love, joy or peace can only be experienced when I can devote my full attention to the moment.

That's when the lights came back on in my head; I'm not a victim of technology—everything I'm doing is by *choice*. I don't have to use it. No one is forcing me to have my BlackBerry with me 24/7, click on that offer, roam Facebook, play electronic solitaire or get sucked into email mania for two hours only to later question why I didn't accomplish what I intended to do that day.

I resolved that I was going to run technology and to stop letting it run me. I started blocking out time in my day specifically for emails, and I created "technology free" time by turning my BlackBerry on silent and staying off the internet. Whenever possible I leave my phone in the car for meetings or when I go out to lunch or dinner.

I build technology breaks into every day. In the early morning or evening I spend at least fifteen minutes outside without my cell phone, which reconnects me with the stillness, beauty and fullness of life. This time helps me recalibrate, focus and strengthen me for whatever challenges await me upon my return. Thanks to this practice, I'm much less vulnerable to the distractions that used to pull me off course.

In the end, if I waste the moments of my life, I waste my life. I don't think anyone will ever be impressed with how many texts or emails I sent or how much time I spent on Facebook. There are a finite number of moments available to me and making the most of them doesn't just matter—it's the only thing that does.

Harbor Lights

The harbor lights of Venus shining,
through the breeze, that brings me back.
—Boz Skaggs

⊢⋅≍♦≍⋅⊣

URING A NINE-HOUR DRIVE from Washington, DC to New
Hampshire I set my iPod on shuffle to help alleviate the boredom
of the ride. When "Harbor Lights" by Boz Skaggs came on, it did
everything but physically transport me back in time to my parents'
living room in Minneapolis in the summer of 1978. "Harbor Lights"
was playing there too and I was telling my friend, Chris "Big C"
Galle, about my girlfriend and that this was "our song."

"Oh man," Big C said wistfully, "you're so lucky. I've always
wanted to have a girlfriend and a song we could call our own." It
was one of the worst things he could have said to me. It was so honest and heartfelt—and it was the exact opposite of what I had just
shared with him. You see, I didn't have a girlfriend, which makes it
highly unlikely that we had a song. As the Baptists might say, I had
just been "convicted."

I was constantly making up stories at that time of my life. If
lying was a felony, I'd still be in prison. I didn't like myself for doing
it, but I know why I did. When my parents moved to Minneapolis

from Massachusetts, I was the new kid in town with a chance to be whoever I wanted to be. I certainly wasn't going to introduce myself as the dork that got beat up every day in junior high school, so I embellished a little.

Okay, okay, I embellished a lot.

Once I realized how easy it was to make things up since no one could fact check anything I had to say, I got really creative. Before long I was everything that I wanted to be—funny, popular, smart and athletic. Girls loved me and boys wanted to be me. It was so absurd that I can laugh about it now, but I couldn't do that before because there was nothing funny to me about being a phony.

My negative self-assessment did motivate me to change my life, but it did not heal me. Whenever I thought about my past I still experienced some degree of guilt, regret or anxiety. Saying to myself, "Art, you were a liar and a cheat," fueled my desire to change—but it was an unhealthy and counter-productive mindset.

The shift came when I read something that Eckhart Tolle wrote in the *Power of Now* cautioning against critical self-evaluation. My first reaction was *what's wrong with that?* A deeper reading of his message helped me see that critical self-judgment (as opposed to self-awareness) adds a negative to a negative—and two negatives will never make a positive.

When I was sixteen I lied, but that doesn't make me a liar or a bad person. I was insecure and my behavior reflected it. My self-judgment was blocking the path to healing. It was only through self-forgiveness and acceptance of the past that I could find the internal peace that I have today.

Reflecting on that moment with Chris made me realize how far I've traveled in my journey. There was a time when I told so many stories I confused myself as to what was the truth and what wasn't. Today I couldn't imagine not being truthful, at least to the extent that I'm aware of it. We all have blind spots and I'm no exception. That's why I'm lucky to have Raquel who unfailingly points those out to me.

I was also struck by how harbor lights are a fitting metaphor of my own search for self-understanding. My voyage has been a lot like a ship at sea, enduring rough waters and storms as I struggled to find my way home. There were many times when I could see the harbor lights in the distance, but something would invariably knock me off course.

But no matter what happened, I kept my hand on the helm and kept steering back to the light. I never lost faith that I would somehow find my way back to the harbor where darkness would finally give way to the light. My journey, of course, is ongoing, but my goal is to keep getting closer to the harbor, where the lights keep getting brighter.

Chris "Big C" Galle and me
Minneapolis, Minnesota–December 1978

You Never Know

Don't judge each day by the harvest you reap,
but by the seeds that you plant
—Robert Louis Stevenson

— ✦ —

I WAS AT A BUSINESS EVENT when I ran into an old friend of mine, Marilyn Balcombe. She gave me a big hug and said, "I have a picture of you hanging up in my closet." I was flabbergasted. The old reporter in me told me there had to be a good story behind this one. After I joked, "Does your husband know?" she told me her story, which would become one of the most unexpected and gratifying moments of my life.

During her battle with breast cancer, Marilyn said my story on running a marathon gave her the inspiration she needed to continue her fight. "I read your story at one of the lowest points in my chemotherapy. I felt like I didn't have any strength left and I wanted to give up," Marilyn said. "But then I just kept saying to myself over and over again what you wrote in that story, *I must finish this race.*"

Marilyn continued her fight and has been cancer free for more than a year now. I was humbled when she told me how much my story inspired her, but the real story is how much she inspired me. My race was voluntary, but for Marilyn cancer wasn't a choice. It was a life or death fight that entered her life without warning.

Her story brings out the depth, meaning and beauty of life in a way that transcends anything I've ever done or written about.

Her battle against this terrible, invisible enemy wasn't just for her. It was for her husband, her daughter and everyone else who knows and loves her. Earlier that year, Marilyn posted a picture on Facebook of her husband Jonathan sporting a freshly-shaved head in a sublime gesture of love and support. In the midst of one of life's scariest trials, love finds a way to bloom and grow.

To see Marilyn so alive and vibrant today is a gratifying reminder of how one word, gesture or act of kindness can make a difference in someone's life. It is a testimony of the power all of us have to touch, inspire, heal, change or motivate others.

Marilyn shared her story with me, but I wonder how many stories are out there that I've never heard. I can't possibly know the extent of my influence, but just knowing that *one action* could help change or save someone's life is enough. One positive gesture can create an endless ripple effect touching and changing lives generations from now.

Marilyn's story to me is a true miracle—and miracles are the magic ingredient of life. Looking back on my journey, I now see that miracles have been with me every step of the way. I couldn't see them at the time because I wasn't looking. I have to look or I'll never see. And the closer I look, the more I see that I am awash in miracles every day.

That's why I start every day with the thought that I can make a difference today. To carry on my quest to keep looking, learning, growing and seeking the truth. Because thanks to people like Marilyn, I know it matters. My journey begins anew every day in the same place it always does, with a willingness to look and change the only thing I can, me.

Jonathan and Marilyn Balcombe
Germantown, Maryland–2010

A True Sailor

—⊹⊰⊱⊹—

SINCE I WAS A BOY I've been fascinated by leaders who inspire people to believe in themselves and achieve things that were said to be "impossible." There were many times that I thought I had found this leader only to be disappointed when his true character was revealed.

My passion for finding the "ideal" leader and my own search for authenticity are closely intertwined. True leaders aren't perfect, but they are authentic. They possess uncommon humility, integrity and an uncompromising passion for doing what's right.

My quest for finding both has been a lifelong exercise in patience, faith and persistence. Leaders of great character are rare, but I never lost hope that I would one day see the vision of my youth in operation.

My faith was rewarded six years ago when I found this leader in Jacksonville, Florida. If you've ever longed to find a leader who touches your heart, renews your faith, and inspires you to believe again—then this is a story for you. I hope you will find it as inspiring reading it as I did witnessing it.

Ironically, after years of searching for this leader, I didn't have to travel far to find her.

Turns out, I was married to her.

Prologue

Keep it simple, be consistent and always be honest.
—Dr. Anatolio B. Cruz, Jr

IN THE TWILIGHT of her tour as the commanding officer of Naval Hospital Jacksonville, Captain Raquel "Rocky" Bono's non-commissioned leadership gave her a statue of a sailor bearing an inscription that read, CAPTAIN ROCKY BONO, A TRUE SAILOR. Those three words convey a rare bond between Rocky and her sailors, an acknowledgment that she is *one of them*—they trust her, stand behind her and will do anything for her.

"I would take her into combat with me anytime," said Master Chief James "Rusty" Perry, a combat veteran who is currently serving in Afghanistan. Perry's praise reflects the highest level of trust and respect that one soldier can give to another. It captures what happens when a leader wins the hearts of his or her followers. And like all great things it is an intangible—an experience of unfathomable power.

I know I cannot give this story the full telling it deserves, but I hope this five-part series on Rocky's three-year tour at the Naval Hospital will offer a glimpse of what Captain Kathy Summers called, "the bravest, most inspiring and courageous leader I have ever known."

Captain Summers said she often wondered how this, "one-hundred pound dynamo," could lead with such grace, heart and courage in the face of adversity and unrelenting pressure. One thing is certain, great character doesn't just happen. It takes years and thousands of hours of dedication and preparation. For Rocky Bono, the forces that shaped her started long before her birth in an archipelago of more than seven thousand islands known as the Philippines.

Just ten hours after the Japanese attack on Pearl Harbor on December 7, 1941, the Imperial Air Force starting raining bombs on the Philippines in preparation for an invasion and occupation that would last for most of World War II. For Raquel's parents, Anatolio "Tony" Cruz and Rosalina "Rose" Sedillo, this chapter of history brought a brutal and premature end to their childhoods.

At the time of the invasion, Tony's father was a reserve officer and a surgeon in the United States Armed Forces in the Far East (USAFFE). He was in Manila, cut off from the main force under the command of General Douglas MacArthur which had retreated to the island fortress of Corregidor. Refusing to sign the Japanese surrender papers, he joined Filipino guerilla forces to serve as a division surgeon.

He was captured and tortured by Japanese soldiers several times, but was freed through the intercession of Tony's mother. In an act of unfathomable bravery she confronted the commander of the dreaded *Kempeitai*, the Japanese military police known for their brutality, and earned his admiration. "My mother could stand up to anybody, no exceptions," Tony recalled.

During the war Raquel's mother lived in Dumaguete on the Japanese-occupied island of Negros Oriental. Her brother, a soldier in the Philippine Army, was lost in one of the early battles, on the Bataan Death March or possibly later in Camp O'Donnell. Tony lost a cousin, and like thousands of Filipinos, they never learned exactly how, or where, they died.

Tony's father divided his time between his home and guerilla forces to maintain an appearance of a normal daily routine. As the oldest of four children, eight-year-old Tony was expected to assume many of his father's responsibilities in his absence, including parenting his four brothers and sisters. He said it was a difficult and painful time, but sacrifices were required of everyone and that they did what they had to in order to survive.

The example his father set of responsibility, commitment and hard work as well as the experience of living on an Army base before the war shaped Tony's character and his ideals. He said that the order, discipline, accountability and precision of military life gave him a practical and effective model for conduct, as well as a deep appreciation for service.

In his words, "I began to understand that to serve one's country is honorable and to do things well is do it with honor and dedication. Courage allows you to accomplish your goals, especially in the face of great odds."

Tony's experiences helped him formulate three inviolable rules for behavior and decisions: 1. Keep it simple. 2. Be consistent. 3. Always be honest. Taken together, these three principles formed one simple, but powerful guide for any life situation—*to always do the right thing*. This is the law he lived his life by and impressed on his children. In matters of principle, there is no gray area for Tony.

After following his father into medicine, earning his medical degree from the College of Medicine, University of the Philippines followed by seven additional years of surgical training in the United States, Dr. Cruz returned to the Philippines to establish his practice and raise his family.

But Tony quickly learned that his approach to medicine was not embraced by the existing culture. If he were to continue practicing there, he would have to compromise his values and principles— something he would never do. So Tony made the most difficult and courageous decision of his life—to leave the country he loved and move his family permanently to the United States.

This was a decision that would greatly benefit the United States through his service and the service of his children. Early in his career

Dr. Cruz developed the Lillehei-Cruz-Kaster artificial heart valve. He played a critical role in the growth of the University of Texas Health Science Center, where he would become the first chief of surgical oncology. He continued the family tradition of military service, joining the United States Navy Reserve, rising to the rank of captain.

Leaving her homeland was a sacrifice for Rose, too. She had to raise four children in a foreign land, far away from her friends, family and support systems. When she appealed to her father-in-law for help, he told her it was her responsibility to "make it work." His counsel was a defining moment in her life. She dedicated herself to raising her children while earning a Masters and a Specialists Degree in Family Therapy on her way to becoming a counselor and family therapist. She *made it work.*

A quiet, humble, immensely intelligent man, Dr. Cruz inspired his children to strive for excellence because he lived it. The oldest of the four children, Raquel was expected from an early age to help take care of her siblings. This instilled a deep appreciation for responsibility, hard work and devotion in her. It taught her the value of selfless service—putting the needs and interests of others above her own.

These ideals inspired both Rocky and her brother, Anatolio "AB" Cruz III, to become naval officers. Rocky was commissioned in 1979 while attending medical school at Texas Tech University. AB earned his commission through the United States Naval Academy and was recently promoted to rear admiral in the United States Navy Reserve.

A unique quality of the Cruz family is that they extend the same loyalty and devotion they have for each other to their community, the Navy, and their country. I was born in the United States and love this country, but I learned more about the true meaning of loyalty, service, and patriotism from my adopted Filipino family than I ever did as a soldier or an American.

Rose and Dr. Anatolio Cruz were indeed the forces that shaped this "one hundred pound dynamo," and for that, they should be immensely proud. Through personal sacrifice, service to others, faith, and, in her father's words, "the bottom line trait, which is the most important, *hard work*," they helped prepare Rocky for the challenge that awaited her.

Anatolio "Tony" Cruz Jr. (center) with his mother, Francisca Fermin Cruz, his father, Colonel Anatolio B. Cruz, with his sister, Ileana Regina, and his grandmother (far left), Damiana Domngo Fermin. Island of Jolo, Philippines–Circa 1936

Captain Anatolio B. Cruz, Jr, Captain Raquel "Rocky" Bono and Captain Anatolio "AB" Cruz III San Antonio, Texas–2008

Honoring the Standard

PART ONE OF FIVE

I will abide by an uncompromising code of integrity,
taking responsibility for my actions and keeping my word.
—From the US Navy Core Value of Honor

———※※———

A S A TRAUMA SURGEON and leader of a casualty receiving unit in Saudi Arabia during the first Gulf War, Captain Raquel "Rocky" Cruz Bono learned early that operational readiness is essential to the Navy's mission. This means that everyone in uniform has to have the proper training, skills, and physical fitness to be ready to deploy in a moment's notice. Operational preparedness to Rocky isn't just a goal—it is a condition of employment for serving your country.

When she began her tour as the commanding officer of the Navy's fourth largest hospital in Jacksonville, Florida, her first priority was to ensure that everyone was meeting or exceeding the Navy's standard for readiness. Using a simple philosophy she adopted from her father, the standards applied to everyone equally. No exceptions.

Rocky's family tradition of military and medical service instilled in her the importance of excellence at a young age. In both professions there is little margin for error—mistakes can cost lives. Excellence matters in everything whether it's performing surgery, cleaning bathrooms, or how people treat each other. Every detail to Rocky is important to the success of the enterprise.

As the first female to complete the general surgery residency program at the Naval Medical Center Portsmouth, Rocky knew that to succeed in a male dominated world she would have to be more than excellent—she would have to work harder, longer, and outperform her peers just to be considered equal.

Above all, she learned that achieving standards of excellence is a matter of honor; personal honor, family honor, and cultural honor. The Navy had the wisdom to establish its core values *Honor, Courage* and *Commitment* from those of its venerable combat division, the United States Marine Corps. In those values, Rocky found the perfect soulmate for her heritage and beliefs.

In the Marines success depends on a shared, near-sacred devotion to the attainment of a higher standard. If a Marine fails to achieve a standard it is viewed as a failure for the individual, the unit he or she serves with, and the entire corps. Every Marine is a part of the whole—and every action contributes to the effectiveness, cohesiveness and integrity of the Marine Corps. Rocky isn't a Marine, but her discipline, toughness, and attention to detail would make them proud to call her one of their own.

But at five feet two and weighing in just north of one hundred pounds, Rocky doesn't just defy a stereotype, she obliterates it. A former Phi Beta Kappa, Summa Cum Laude student and Junior Olympic swimmer, her mercurial beauty, thousand-watt smile and razor-sharp intellect can instantly neutralize the toughest opponents. She's a paradoxical combination of a combat officer with a heart of gold.

From day one in Jacksonville, she personally led early morning training runs and *encouraged* me to join her. Her senior enlisted leader, Command Master Chief Sylve, delightfully said it was the first time he'd seen that in his thirty-year career. "Man, if she can get her *husband* up at that hour, then I'm not taking any excuses from my sailors. I'm putting the word out right now." The next week, attendance soared from fifty to more than two hundred and stayed there for the duration of her three-year command.

The word got out quickly—if you were stationed in Jacksonville—you had better get with the program. The skipper, as Navy commanders are affectionately called, would give anyone the opportunity to meet the standards and do everything she could to help them get there, but she would never compromise the standards themselves. The practice of granting waivers or making exceptions was over.

Sailors violating rules of conduct could accept the punishment determined by their leadership or they could appeal through Captain's Mast, a non-judicial proceeding run by the commanding officer. If defendants were honest, humble, and willing to correct their mistakes, Rocky could be empathetic, lenient and generous with second chances.

If they were defensive, belligerent or dishonest, they could expect a grilling that makes Judge Judy look like a vacuous teenager. Using questions sharper than the surgeon's scalpel she used to wield, she'd get to the truth faster than a water boarding. The vocabulary of even the most recalcitrant sailors was quickly reduced to three words, "Yes or no, ma'am."

"She was always so attentive and personable with everyone," recalled Captain Darin Rogers, her director for administration and a former starting linebacker for West Virginia, "but if you crossed her or tried to lie to her, someone had better get the chaplain. (When provoked), she could knock down an elephant."

As dedicated as she was to ensuring everyone met the standards, Rocky saw the standard as a *minimum* level of performance. The true standard, to her, was bringing out the very best of everyone in her command and far exceeding any existing level of performance. "She set the bar way high," recalls Captain Kathy Summers. "But she inspired me to over-deliver for her. I couldn't wait to get to that bar and jump over it."

The test of Rocky's dedication to maintaining standards came less than a year into her tour. Her new executive officer (second-in-command) reported in with a letter from the command school advising

Rocky that they were unable to certify her completion of the course because she failed to meet the minimum weight standard.

Rocky was in an untenable position. If she allowed this officer, whom she knew and respected, to assume her duties, it meant that the second highest ranking officer in the command would be responsible for enforcing standards that she couldn't maintain herself. It would jeopardize the integrity of everything she was working toward.

But to seek a replacement would disrupt the selection process, which could have adverse ramifications for the officer's career—and Rocky's, too. The personal risks were high, but they weren't a consideration for Rocky because the standards to her are inviolable. They are the foundation of honor, courage and commitment—the fabric of character—and to compromise them would dishonor the Navy, herself, her family, and everyone in the command who worked and sacrificed to maintain the minimum fitness level.

Rocky told the officer how personally difficult this was, but that she had to act in the best interests of the entire command and that she was going to request a replacement for her. This decision rocked the naval medical community. As far as anyone could remember, something like this had never been done before.

But her decision had an unexpected result that bordered on miraculous; it created a rebirth of faith among her non-commissioned officers who had long since been disillusioned or demoralized by officers who held them accountable for enforcing standards that they wouldn't enforce within their own community. "I loved everything she was doing, but I was still holding back because I'd been burned too many times," Master Chief Perry said to me. "But when she took that stand…that did it. I was sold for life."

To her master chiefs, senior chiefs and petty officers, Rocky was the leader they longed for—the embodiment of everything they believed the Navy could be back in their youth when their idealism was intact and untarnished. And when she backed up her words with action, without regard to personal consequences, they knew they had finally found a leader they could trust and believe in. Their faith in the Navy, and everything it represents was restored.

Raquel restored my faith, too. When I resigned my commission from the reserves, a significant factor in that decision was my disillusionment with a culture where principles were often sacrificed in the interest of career advancement. I didn't like what was happening in practice, but I never lost faith in what the spine-tingling power of ideals such as *honor, courage* and *commitment* can do when we dedicate ourselves to living them through our actions.

Rocky taught me that uncompromising dedication to standards is not only possible, but essential to elevate our life and the lives of others. Those standards apply to everything and everyone. If I wouldn't want a surgeon to cut corners, or my local restaurant to lower health standards, or my housekeeper to be satisfied with a partially clean house, then I need to expect the best of myself in whatever I do.

As for Rocky's team in Jacksonville, their commitment to readiness and their faith in their leader would be critical in the months ahead, as Naval Hospital Jacksonville was about to face its greatest test.

Rocky going through a medical combat obstacle course.
Jacksonville, Florida–March 2007

Courage Under Fire
PART TWO OF FIVE

I will make decisions in the best interest of the Navy and the nation, without regard to personal consequences.
—FROM THE US NAVY CORE VALUE OF COURAGE

W HEN ROCKY ASSUMED COMMAND of Naval Hospital Jacksonville, she was singularly focused on fulfilling her life's passion—to create one of the finest health-care systems in the world—a place of healing and wellness where every decision begins and ends with the best interests of the patient in mind. What she couldn't foresee was that events were already in motion that would soon place her at the epicenter of one of the fiercest storms in recent Navy medicine history.

There are moments of history, however, when lives and events intersect in such perfect synchronization that it seems as if both were created, long ago, for that one moment in time. Rocky didn't seek or ask to be given this challenge, but it brought out her talents and abilities in such a way that it would leave no doubt she was destined for it.

In October 2005, just two months into her tour, a federal judge levied a $61 million dollar judgment against Naval Hospital Jacksonville. The penalty, thought to be the highest medical malpractice judgment in federal government history, was the opening act in a maelstrom of negative publicity that would besiege the hospital for the next two years.

In the months following the verdict, Sean Cronin, the malpractice attorney who represented the family, launched a series of lawsuits against the hospital, announcing each one in press conferences at the end of the day, giving the hospital little or no time to respond before the story ran. Using brief excerpts taken from huge medical records, Cronin made shocking allegations including assertions that doctors were using "dirty instruments" on patients. The media reported many of these charges as the lead story without verification or review of the medical records.

Although the facts would ultimately reveal that many of the allegations were misleading, distorted or untrue, the hospital was unable to respond due to patient privacy laws or legal restrictions on active lawsuits, which prevented the release of records or the discussion of specific cases. When pressed by the media, the hospital's initial reticence contributed to a perception that it had something to hide.

True or not, the negative publicity forced the hospital to contend with a firestorm of questions and demands for explanations from Navy headquarters, patients, community leaders, and US congressman and senators. It seemed everyone wanted to know the answer to one question: "What is going on at Jacksonville Naval Hospital?"

At the height of the controversy, the *Navy Times*, a non-official but influential weekly newspaper distributed to Navy personnel throughout the world, published a front page story excoriating Jacksonville Naval Hospital titled, Bad Medicine. In one of the few bright moments of that difficult time, CNO Michael Mullen, the Navy's top admiral, told Navy Surgeon General Don Arthur that he wasn't worried about Jacksonville because, "Rocky Bono's got that."

Under intense pressure from every direction, Rocky's first response was to keep her leadership and everyone at the hospital focused on the mission. "She said our patients come first," recalled her executive officer and current Rear Admiral Elaine Wagner. "She kept us locked-in and focused on our mission, which was to ensure we were operationally prepared to meet the needs of the Navy and to provide patients with the finest, family-centered care possible."

Displaying a trait she inherited from her mother, Rocky's "no excuses" mindset would serve her well. When any new allegation surfaced against the hospital, no matter how outrageous or untrue it was, Rocky had only two questions for her leadership: 1) What can we learn from this? 2) How will this make us better? There was zero tolerance for self-pity or finger-pointing. She kept her command focused like a laser beam on readiness, patient care and safety—and never let up.

With her team focusing on their patients, Rocky turned her attention to the fight. Sean Cronin was about to get schooled on why they call this diminutive Filipina surgeon, "Rocky." In a decision that defines her, Rocky did the most audacious and unexpected thing. Rejecting the counsel of her legal team to hunker down, Rocky made a commitment to total transparency.

With the fate of the hospital she loved and her career on the line, her decision was thought by some to be ill-advised or even reckless. But the principles she was raised with didn't allow for any other option. Rocky's principles don't wilt under pressure; if anything, they grow stronger. And with her father's wisdom whispering in her ear, *never do anything that compromises who you are*, Rocky went into battle with the only weapon she needed, the truth.

The truth that Rocky would bet her reputation on is that Naval Hospital Jacksonville was one of the finest hospitals in the world. Its patient safety record consistently scored fifty-percent better than the national average. Moreover, the same men and women who were delivering the highest life-saving rates in history on the battlefields in Iraq and Afghanistan were serving their patients in Jacksonville.

Rocky didn't resist closer scrutiny, she welcomed it. So to Sean Cronin, the media, or anyone else who impugned or maligned the reputation of the doctors, nurses and corpsmen whose only crime was to dedicate their lives to serving their country, she had one message for them: Bring it on.

She invited the media in for interviews and/or to inspect the hospital; she offered to meet with the patients who were suing the hospital; she maintained an open door policy for *any patient* wishing to see her; she held town meetings for the community and patients; she held question and answer sessions with every business, civic or community group in the Jacksonville area; and she developed and led patient safety training seminars for everyone in her command.

Had she listened to her legal advice, she would have missed her chance to meet with a patient who told Rocky how honored he was that she would meet with him personally and that he didn't even want to sue the hospital. The real issue was that he was grieving the loss of his wife. Rocky told him how sorry she was for his loss, which gave him what he really wanted, someone to share in his grief and pain.

Then Captain Rocky Bono did the unthinkable; she called the Joint Commission on Accreditation and requested a full review of the hospital. Commission officials didn't know how to respond—they said it was the first time anyone had *requested* a review. The commission typically inspects hospitals at random, something that keeps CEOs up at night because the results have the potential to damage its reputation or endanger its accreditation. Asking for an inspection is like calling the IRS and saying, "Would you please give me an audit?"

During all of these meetings or investigations, Rocky never had a lawyer with her, never used prepared scripts and answered every question—unless it violated patient privacy laws—honestly and completely. Every case she had to defend occurred before her tenure as the commanding officer, but she never once complained or felt sorry for herself, publicly or privately.

When the storm was at its worst Rocky was at her best, doing what all great captains do in times of crisis. She kept her hand firmly on the helm, keeping the ship on course no matter what obstacles came their way. "She was the calm in the storm," recalled Master Chief Perry. "She had a special quality—calm, cool and collected on the outside and a tough warrior on the inside. She was quick, firm, fair, and professional in every aspect of her leadership."

In a display of courage reminiscent of her grandmother's confrontation of a Japanese interrogator in the Philippines in World War II, Rocky inspired and uplifted an entire command. She exemplified the Navy's core value of courage, which it defines, in part, as the ability to "make decisions in the best interest of the Navy and the nation, without regard to personal consequences...courage is the value that gives us the moral and mental strength to do what is right, even in the face of personal or professional adversity."

I learned many things from Rocky's stand in Jacksonville, but the enduring lesson for me is nothing can defeat the truth if we have the faith and the courage to tell it. Since she was a young girl, her father impressed on her the importance of *always being honest*. And always doesn't mean most of the time, it means all the time. Truth may take a beating in the short term, but it will always win the war.

Since Rocky always told the truth her testimony was authentic, credible and believable. Reporters and investigators searched for gaps or inconsistencies, but couldn't find them. It took time, but they inexorably found themselves pulled to the only viable conclusion, that many of the allegations were exaggerated or simply not true. It wasn't that adverse outcomes didn't occur, or that the hospital was blameless, but malpractice was not a systemic problem.

The truth restored Jacksonville Naval Hospital's rightful reputation. By the time Rocky rotated out of command in the summer of 2008, Naval Hospital Jacksonville had never been stronger. She had the full support of Navy medicine, her patients, the local community,

Congress and even the media. And the bewildered Joint Commission did accede to Rocky's request for a review and, after just a few recommendations for improvement, gave Jacksonville Naval Hospital its highest rating.

Photos by PH3 David Didier

Retired Army Sgt. Demos Johnson expresses his gratitude to Naval Hospital Jacksonville Commanding Officer Capt. Raquel Bono for the care he receives at the hospital during a town hall meeting Jan. 18.

Rocky answers questions at a Town Meeting
Jacksonville, Florida–January 2007

An Unconditional Commitment

PART THREE OF FIVE

I will care for the safety, professional,
personal and spiritual well-being of our people.
—FROM THE US NAVY CORE VALUE OF COMMITMENT

TWO YEARS INTO HER COMMAND, Rocky heard a story that turned her blood cold. A former Jacksonville psychiatrist, Dr. Heidi Kraft, the author of *Rule Number Two*, gave a personal account of her experience treating soldiers in Iraq. On stage in front of two hundred people she recounted the pain and loneliness she experienced when she arrived at the airport after a deployment and no one from the Navy was there to help her or even welcome her home.

After her talk, Rocky told Dr. Kraft how sorry she was for her experience and even though she couldn't erase it, Rocky assured her that things had changed in Jacksonville. She told her about her Yellow Ribbon program that not only recognized and supported every sailor before, during and after deployment, but their families as well. Moreover, she told her that it was an issue of such importance, that she made a commitment to personally attend every deployment send-off and return that she possibly could—and she challenged her leadership to do the same.

When Rocky made that commitment I applauded her devotion, but wondered how she could possibly keep it given that fifteen percent of the four thousand sailors in her command were deployed on a continuous basis. I've since learned that Rocky doesn't accept that kind of thinking. It's not that she doesn't see, understand or appreciate the challenges; it's simply that the value of the action outweighs any obstacle or sacrifice.

What I didn't know then was that her command was more than her responsibility, it was *her family.* She could no sooner send them into harm's way without being there than she would her own child. And for this fiercely loyal Filipina, she ensured that her commitment to her sailors didn't come at the expense of her children—she almost never missed a game, performance, teacher conference or other significant event in her children's lives.

When sailors were deploying, the last thing Rocky did at the airport was to reassure them of her commitment to their families. "We want you to concentrate on saving the lives of our brave sailors and Marines," Rocky told them. "We promise to take care of your families. We'll all be praying for you and waiting for your safe return."

Rocky kept her promise to them and continued to make late night and early morning trips to the airport even while she was consumed by the media and investigations stemming from the malpractice lawsuits against the hospital. According to Rocky's code, a commitment is a commitment—and nothing was going to stop her from fulfilling it. After two years, however, these trips did take a toll.

During one challenging stretch, I asked Raquel why she didn't delegate more often. Without hesitation, she said, "Because these people are sacrificing so much, including leaving their families to go into hostile areas and save lives, the least I can do is sacrifice a few hours of sleep to send them off and welcome them home." That was the last objection she ever heard from me about that.

To her command, Rocky's stamina was superhuman, but what they never saw were the times when she would get home late at night after a grueling week and collapse on the couch, her body being the only thing that could betray her. One Friday night, I carried her up to bed, ensuring the alarm was set for another early morning trip to the airport.

Rocky woke up the next morning feeling sick and exhausted. She said something I had never heard her say before, "I'm not sure I can do this." As she struggled to find the strength to get up, she remembered that no one else from her leadership team was scheduled to be there. This gave her the emotional fuel to override her illness, put on her uniform and go.

When she arrived a junior enlisted sailor who was deploying that morning broke into a huge smile and ran into her arms exclaiming, "Oh Captain Bono! I was just telling everyone here that I *knew* you would come to see me off." It turned out that she had been bragging to her friends and family that the commanding officer was going to be there to see her personally.

Despite demands and pressures that might crush ordinary mortals, Rocky kept her promise. She did something that has endeared people to their leaders throughout history; she put their needs and interests above her own. She is a living example of the Navy core value of commitment which it defines, in part, "to treat each individual with human dignity; be committed to positive change and constant improvement; exhibit the highest degree of moral character."

The decision she made was unconditional, which meant that *no condition*, event or circumstance could justify abandoning it. The enduring lesson for me, having witnessed the unbridled elation of her doctors, nurses and corpsmen when they saw her waiting for them at the end of the jetway, is the power and importance of a true commitment. I also realized how easy it is to break commitments when I start to rationalize things based on how I *feel* and not by what is *right*.

Whenever I feel the urge to succumb to my own needs or interests, I think of what might have happened to that young sailor if Raquel had listened to my advice to stay home. I picture her standing there until the last minute, finally turning to walk down the jetway alone, her spirit crushed as she begins a six thousand mile trip to a dangerous, hostile land.

Rocky's commitment to the Navy, her country, her command, and to her family, defines commitment. There were so many times Rocky could have delegated, as I once suggested, or have given in to the powerful human pull for more sleep, but she believed their sacrifice was much greater than hers. And, to Rocky, a commitment is more than a decision; it's an unchangeable part of her character.

Rocky sending off her sailors to deployment
Jacksonville, Florida–September 2007

Simple Gestures

PART FOUR OF FIVE

We cannot do great things, only small things with great love.
—Mother Teresa

O NE OF THE FIRST THINGS Rocky did when she assumed command of the hospital was call the head of the cleaning department, Annette Brown, and asked to meet with her. Mrs. Brown asked her what time she should report to her office and Rocky surprised her by telling her that she wanted to come to her. Ten minutes later Rocky met her in an office not much bigger than a closet.

Rocky told Annette how much she valued and appreciated the work she and her staff put in every day to keep the hospital clean. "I know that we both understand that how the hospital looks creates a first impression on patients," Rocky said, "which lifts their spirits; a small, but essential part of their confidence in the care we give them."

With tears in her eyes, Mrs. Brown replied, "Ma'am, I've worked here twenty-one years and no one has ever visited me here or thanked us for what we do." In a spontaneous burst of affection, she hugged Rocky and whispered in her ear, "Ma'am, you'll never need to worry about the cleanliness of this hospital. We are going to take good care of *you*."

Six months later, Don Arthur, the surgeon general of the United States Navy, toured the hospital on an official visit and commented that he's been to nearly every Naval medical facility in the world and Jacksonville was the cleanest he's ever seen. Eschewing any credit for herself, Rocky quickly arranged for the entire cleaning staff to have their picture taken with the surgeon general.

"That's one of the miracles of Captain Bono's leadership," said her director for administration, Captain Darin Rogers. "She'd shine the light on people who had never been recognized before in their entire lives. People would come up to me with tears in their eyes and tell me how much she meant to them. I swear they'd take a bullet for her."

Rogers went on to say that Rocky reached out to everyone in every corner of the hospital; she'd serve meals with the junior enlisted, visit engineers in the basement, get on the roof with facilities personnel or spend time with data entry people in remote areas of the building; always taking a personal interest in their lives and never forgetting to tell them how grateful she was for their service.

When the hospital experienced severe power loss during a storm one weekend, contractors worked for seventy-two hours straight to keep the generators going so the hospital could keep running equipment and perform operations. Afterward Rocky arranged for a special ceremony, where she told them that she couldn't give them back the time they lost with their families, but that they were heroes to her and she would never forget it. Prohibited by law to give gifts to contractors, she awarded each of them a ceremonial command coin that she paid for out of personal funds.

As I reflect on these moments, I am amazed by the power of one small gesture of appreciation. Mrs. Brown faithfully served her country for more than two decades, serving under at least eight different commanding officers, and not once had she received recognition or appreciation. And then one day the phone rings, followed by a two-minute meeting that fills her heart with the one thing she longed to hear, that her work is valued and appreciated.

I also thought about how often I overlook the people who do the work I take for granted—the people doing the so-called thankless work like sanitation, construction, meat packing, etc., who quietly provide the services essential to our way of life. Her leadership reminds me to keep appreciation in my thoughts and in my heart, and to express that whenever possible. And to remember that regardless of the service we provide, *everything we do matters*.

It mattered to Annette Brown. Two years later, she wrote a letter to Rocky, telling her, "You are the most remarkable person I have ever met. I often hear our staff asking about you and reminiscing about the gratitude and kindness you expressed to them. We are still feeling the positive effect you had on our customers and we continue to benefit from everything you taught us. Words cannot express the love and appreciation we have for you."

Rocky and Annette Brown
Jacksonville, Florida–April 2010

The Right Thing

CONCLUSION OF FIVE-PART SERIES

Leadership is love.
—JOHN MAXWELL

———※✦※———

ONE OF ROCKY'S ABSOLUTES was her open door policy for any patient who wanted to see her. As her executive assistant Dana Myers could attest, this commitment created scheduling nightmares, but Rocky wanted to send the strongest message possible to her staff that patients are their highest priority. But her ultimate goal for her caregivers went even higher than that—she wanted them to treat, care for and listen to their patients with *love*.

To love patients Rocky believed her staff needed to understand them. She established an instant electronic customer feedback system and ensured that every concern, no matter how seemingly petty or small, was addressed. "I want to hear every one of these complaints," she told her executive team. "We need to dig down deep. We have to know if we're meeting their needs."

One of her patients met with Rocky after her doctors and nurses refused to change the terminology on a highly sensitive medical procedure. The medical staff defended its decision because it was technically correct, but the issue for Rocky was that one of their patients

217

was suffering emotionally and her staff just wasn't, in her words, "getting it." So she set up a meeting with every caregiver involved in this patient's care so they could personally listen to her story.

In heartbreaking detail the patient described how cold and devastated she felt seeing the terminology the hospital used to describe her procedure. Caregivers present for that meeting later said there wasn't a dry eye in the room. When she was finished, they couldn't change the language on the chart fast enough. "It was a humbling experience," one participant said. "Talking about love is one thing, but this made it so real...it brought home everything the skipper was trying to get us to understand about loving patients."

Although love may have been the main ingredient, it was her consistency that built the loyalty, respect, and devotion of her command. Rocky was consistent because no matter how difficult, unpopular, or even personally damaging it was, she *always did the right thing*. One of her bedrock beliefs was to never pass the buck. If there was something that needed to be done, then she needed to do it, regardless of the cost.

When Navy medicine needed to send a large team to the detainee prison at Guantanamo Bay, Cuba, Rocky volunteered her command even though they were already stretched thin with deployments to Iraq and Afghanistan. Guantanamo was a tough, unpopular assignment so her staff avoided putting more senior and experienced personnel on the list. When Rocky saw this, she immediately rejected it, telling them, "I know this is a difficult assignment, which is exactly why we need to send our best, brightest and most experienced people."

So they sent their best people, including then-Commander Darin Rogers to command the clinic. While they were deployed, not only did Rocky visit them, but she insisted on serving alongside her staff as they delivered care to detainees, who would taunt, intimidate and sometimes attack their caregivers. "If they're going to endure that, then they need to know that I'm right there with them," Rocky said.

At the end of a fiscal year, her comptroller told her the hospital had a surplus of $10 million and asked her what she wanted to do with it. The answer she gave him was one he never expected to hear: "Give it back to Navy medicine."

Her unyielding commitment to doing the right thing gave her command something they longed for in a leader—a *certainty* that they could trust her to consistently act in the best interests of everyone concerned. They found a leader who didn't shift when the winds changed or when things got tough. She didn't play favorites, make closed-door deals, or do anything out of self-interest. Her decisions weren't always popular, but her motives were never in doubt.

In Rocky Bono, Naval Hospital Jacksonville found leader who gave them unconditional love and high expectations. She inspired them to achieve things far beyond anything they had ever thought possible. She created a community that grew to love and serve their patients, outperform expectations and care for each other. She put their needs above hers, and in return, they gave her everything they had.

Leadership is a complex subject, and yet I can easily summarize the secret to Rocky's success in one word, *character*. Rocky didn't use textbook leadership techniques because her character transcended them. She is a living testimony to everything that *honor*, *courage* and *commitment* is, can and should be.

She restored my faith in the power, promise and truth of ideals that are far too often sacrificed out of ignorance, weakness or self-interest—and she proved, beyond any doubt, that the power of refusing to compromise those ideals is far stronger than any force that opposes it.

Rocky often told her staff about the importance of action and how their influence creates ripples that have the potential to change lives now and possibly forever. Rocky created a ripple that continues to live on in the lives of the men and women she touched during her time in Jacksonville. And for that she earned the only praise that really matters, that she is now and always will be *A True Sailor*.

Epilogue

—·—⊱◈⊰—·—

ON APRIL 21, 2011, Raquel "Rocky" Bono was selected for the rank of Rear Admiral in the United States Navy. She is the first female trauma surgeon and only the third Filipina to attain this rank in US Navy history.

Rocky and her brother, AB Cruz III, will be the first brother/sister combination of Filipino descent to serve as flag officers at the same time.

Rear Admiral (Select) Raquel "Rocky" Bono
Washington, DC–May 2011

About the Author

ART DWIGHT is a writer, speaker and personal coach. He lives in Alexandria, Virginia. To learn more about Art, or to book him for speaking engagements, go to:

www.ArtDwight.com

CPSIA information can be obtained
at www.ICGtesting.com
Printed in the USA
LVHW01s0241141117
556190LV00001B/148/P